THE PAST AS FUTURE

»THE PAST«
»AS«
»FUTURE«

»Vergangenheit als Zukunft«

JÜRGEN HABERMAS

Interviewed by Michael Haller

Translated & edited by Max Pensky

Foreword by Peter Hohendahl

University of Nebraska Press

Lincoln & London

1994

Originally published
as *Vergangenheit als Zukunft: Das
alte Deutschland
im neuen Europa?* Copyright © by pendo-
verlag, Zürich 1991
© 1994 by the University of Nebraska Press
Set in Berkeley
by Keystone Typesetting, Inc.
Design: RE

Library of Congress Cataloging in Publication Data
Habermas, Jürgen. [Vergangenheit als Zukunft. English]
The past as future: Vergangenheit als Zukunft / by Jürgen
Habermas; interviewed by Michael Haller; translated and
edited by Max Pensky; foreword by Peter Hohendahl.
p. cm. – (Modern German culture and literature series)
Includes bibliographical references and index.
ISBN 0-8032-2371-4 (cloth: alk. paper). – ISBN 0-8032-7266-9
(pbk.: alk. paper) 1. Germany – History – 1990 – 2. Political
culture – Germany. 3. National characteristics, German.
4. Persian Gulf War, 1991 – Germany. 5. Germany – Politics
and government – 1900 –   6. Germany – History –
Philosophy. I. Haller, Michael, 1945–. II. Title. III. Series.
DD290.29.H313 1994 943.087'9 – dc 20 93-32385 CIP

Contents

Foreword by Peter Hohendahl

Among the numerous interviews Jürgen Habermas has given during the last decade or so, *The Past as Future* stands out for more than one reason. It is not only his most extensive dialogue to date but also his most carefully prepared exchange of questions and answers. Michael Haller, the interviewer, submitted his questions in writing, thereby giving Habermas time to go beyond an immediate response and to reflect on the broader ramifications of the subject. The interview presents itself as a *tour d'horizon* of the German intellectual scene of the early 1990s, ranging from the heated debate about the Gulf War and its meaning for German politics to a discussion about changing theoretical paradigms during the 1980s. Among the issues that Habermas treats extensively we also find the question of the collapse of state socialism in East Germany and the new German identity after the unification of 1990. Here Habermas picks up and continues arguments that he developed in a number of important essays published during the 1980s.[1] At that time he intervened in the German Historians' Debate as well as the acrimonious dispute about German unification. That Habermas spoke out about the use of German history, especially objecting to the so-called normalization of the German past, angered his conservative opponents. One of their rhetorical devices to undermine his position was the charge that he, as a mere philosopher, was not qualified to discuss historical topics.[2] In the best German Mandarin tradition they set up a sharp

vii

distinction between professional historians and nonex-
perts, who were not legitimized to speak. What made Habermas's essays and interviews particularly offensive in the
eyes of his adversaries was his claim to address subjects that
were outside his professorial expertise.

In other words, *The Past as Future,* like Habermas's political writings of the 1980s, raises the broader question of the
status of the intellectual and his or her role in the public
sphere. Quite consciously, Habermas has claimed the role
of the intellectual for himself and deliberately transcended
the boundaries of his academic appointment. Accordingly,
he has played a role in German intellectual life that his
American readers by and large have not fully appreciated.
The role of the intellectual is based on free and immediate
access to the media of mass communication. It presupposes
the existence of a general public sphere as a forum for intellectual exchange, an exchange of opinions and arguments
that ought to be accessible to the general public. For this
reason, Habermas's interviews are written in a style quite
different from that of his theoretical works – less technical
and more colloquial. Although Habermas clearly follows
the tradition of the Frankfurt school, especially Theodor
Adorno and Herbert Marcuse, his style of communication
does not use the essay form as it was developed by Adorno.
While the Adornian essay tends to move toward the bor-
derline of rational language, Habermas clearly prefers a di-
alogical model – one reason why he has been more comfortable with the interview format than Adorno. For Habermas, the role of the intellectual is, as he explains in his essay
'Heinrich Heine and the Intellectual in Germany,' historically specific. The intellectual is a European phenomenon
of the late nineteenth and early twentieth centuries, one

that presupposes the existence of a fully developed political public sphere. The intellectual who establishes him- or herself as a spokesperson of public causes outside the acknowledged political institutions becomes the defender of causes for which no appropriate voice could be found in the arena of official political life. Habermas sees the intellectual in a supplemental function, as someone who counters and subverts the hegemonic discourse.

To be sure, Habermas's insistence on the importance of the intellectual has to be seen within the German context, where the conventional definition of the political sphere, at least until after World War II, tended to exclude nonprofessional interventions or at least made them suspicious. The apolitical tradition within the German academy has been stronger than in the West, making it more difficult to define the proper public role of the intellectual. Habermas rejects both the apolitical tradition of German high culture and the strictly professional and institutional definition of politics (Realpolitik). But he also dismisses the confusion of 'intellectual influence within a democratic public sphere with possession of political power'[3] in the case of political activists. Thus Heinrich Heine, though historically a precursor of the modern intellectual, remains in more than one respect Habermas's model: an unorthodox participant in the philosophical and political debates of his times, yet without a claim to power or absolute truth. What Habermas admires in Heine's prose is its qualified radicalism, that is, its reliance on the publicity of the intellectual debate and its dependence on the spirit of critical enlightenment. Detached critical activity is the formula for the paradigm that Habermas prescribes for the contemporary intellectual. Clearly, for Habermas, modern democracy is unthinkable without intellectuals, not because they are endowed with a form of higher truth or with special powers, but because their task is to influence public debate through arguments and criticism. This definition undercuts the recent distinction between universal and special intellectuals introduced by Michel Foucault in his critique of Jean-Paul Sartre. While Habermas seems to uphold a more emphatic understanding of the role of the intellectual than does Foucault, he carefully avoids the representative function that the French tradition had claimed for the intellectual.

Habermas's responses to his interviewer's questions practice this definition of a debate among intellectuals. Michael Haller, an author and journalist, comes across as a sympathetic interviewer, someone who shares common ground with Habermas. Still, their positions are by no means identical. Haller's questions articulate a more skeptical and less systematic approach. He is possibly more sympathetic to the changes in Germany's intellectual and cultural climate in the years after the fall of the Berlin Wall. These shifts, less visible in the first part of the interview (covering the Gulf War), become more pronounced in Haller's remarks in the third part (dealing with the German question) and the last section (taking up theory). Haller's opening remarks to the final chapter articulate his belief that the theoretical configuration of the 1960s and 1970s, dominated by Critical Theory, is no longer available in the public sphere. While Habermas's response tries to downplay the significance of *Theoriemüdigkeit* (weariness with theory) in Germany, Haller seems to share a postmodern attitude of resignation, a lack of belief in historical development that one might find among members of a younger generation. Thus Haller's weariness with theory (which Habermas does not share at all) might possibly be read as a weariness with specific forms of theory, such as Critical Theory and its implicit utopian dimension. In short, what makes the dialogue between Haller and Habermas interesting is precisely their open and hidden disagreements, which result in provocative questions and force Habermas to define his own position within the German intellectual sphere.

GERMANY AND THE GULF WAR

Although Germany was not directly involved in the Gulf War and limited its support to financial and diplomatic aid, the outbreak of the war and the ensuing military actions led to a heated debate, which divided the German public as much as a similar discussion divided the American people. The German debate shaped up in a somewhat different way, however. It focused on issues that were of lesser importance in the American discussion – for instance, the involvement of German industry in providing Iraq with chemical weapons and parts for the missiles that were used to attack Israel. Moreover, the fact that Israel was drawn into the conflict (while militarily handicapped to defend itself) became a major issue in the German debate. In contrast, the plans and strategies of the Bush administration, as well as the American discussion that preceded the war (especially the opposition to the war), was less visible in Germany.

One of the important consequences of the German debate was the further breakup of the German left, which had begun in 1989 in the dispute over the collapse of state socialism in East Germany. While the German left had been united in its opposition to Vietnam, it could not find a common ground in the case of the Gulf War. Those who opposed the war either argued that the conflict had little to do with the freedom of Kuwait and was carried out to secure economic interests of the West, or they assumed that the United States used the Kuwait question to reshape the balance of power in the Middle East. The voices in favor of the war used either principled arguments – for instance, a description of Saddam Hussein as an evil force that had to be eliminated – or they relied on more specific arguments, such as the intolerable threat to Israel's security. In short, the evaluation of the war and the way in which it was carried out largely depended on the perception of the character of the underlying conflict, the rights of the agents on both sides, the war's moral and political context, and its historical background.

Habermas's contribution to this debate is marked by a cautious rational detachment – more specifically, by an attempt to separate overlapping issues, which caused a great deal of confusion in the German media. While he had expressed himself very polemically in the debate on Germany's past, his treatment of the Gulf War emphasizes the task of analyzing the conflicting problems and issues.

Habermas distinguishes four levels: (1) the dimension of power politics, that is, the West's interest in having access to the oil and Iraq's interest in controlling more of the available oil reserves for its economic and political gain; (2) the dimension of the colonial past that haunts the West; (3) the dimension of modern warfare, that is, the use of chemical weapons and advanced technologies to carry out air raids; and (4) the moral dimension of the war, namely, the quest for peace through and by the United Nations.

Habermas's own contributions to these four dimensions are unevenly distributed. While he certainly considers the aspect of power politics and the historical dimension of the war, he is most keenly interested in the fourth aspect of the conflict. Much of his own discussion focuses on the question of legitimacy: to what extent was the Gulf War justified as a legitimate military action carried out by the United States and its allies on behalf of the United Nations? There are two reasons for this emphasis: Habermas's refusal to see the war primarily or exclusively as an instrument of raw power politics, and second, his broader interest in the possibility of an international peacekeeping force that will ultimately transform the nature of foreign relations. It is clearly the theoretical question, as it was raised in Kant's treatise 'On Perpetual Peace,' that informs his discussion of the Gulf War. Hence the aspect that sways Habermas to accept the war as a legitimate military action is Iraq's violation of international law.

GERMAN UNIFICATION

German neonationalism, which slowly but strongly re-emerged during the 1980s and redefined national politics after 1989, has denounced its opponents as a group of mal-adjusted leftists: members of the former student movement, academics and journalists with strong ties to the former German Democratic Republic, and dogmatic liberals who tend to confuse the nation with its constitution.[4] Hence any critique of German unification as the basis for a renewed concept of nationalist policies has been labeled as inappropriate. This distinction between good and bad forces has conveniently served to marginalize the German left, which does not easily fit into the categories put forth by the neonationalists (who themselves are of course a rather heterogeneous group). Habermas's resistance to German unification, for instance, was not linked to a defense of the former German Democratic Republic and its form of state socialism. In fact, Habermas leaves no doubt about his distance from the GDR. Very much in the tradition of the Frankfurt school, he completely rejects the orthodox Marxism of the East German state and is quite critical of its repressive political regime. In this respect, but in this one only, he concurs with the neoconservative forces who celebrated the collapse of the GDR as a victory of Western freedom.

Habermas's resistance to German unification was motivated by two concerns: first, a procedural concern about the process of the unification, and second, a broader concern about the character of the united Germany as a democratic nation. The procedural question whether unification should be achieved according to Article 23 or Article 146 of the Basic Law – that is, through the incorporation of the former GDR in the Federal Republic or through a formal reconstitution of the German nation[5] – implies the fundamental issue of the moral and legal character of the reconstituted German Republic. Habermas clearly favors the demand for a new constitution, as it was articulated in Article 146 of the Basic Law, arguing that German democracy would be strengthened by a constitution that was supported by the entire nation. For Habermas, the question of German nationalism should focus on the political rights of the citizens granted by the constitution rather than a common ethnic and cultural background. His position implies an unmistakable rejection of any form of traditional nationalism as it was proposed by the neoconservatives.

Habermas's critique of German nationalism is not so much a disapproval of the nation-state, as some of his opponents have suspected, as a critique of an ethnic and cultural grounding of the national community. The conflation of political and ethnic or cultural boundaries is perceived as a danger to a democratic political order. In the recent German debate about the rights of foreigners asking for asylum and the rights of the so-called guest workers, this conflation has become a crucial issue. Those who want to change the German constitution in order to stop the influx of asylum seekers have argued for the priority of an ethnically bounded Germany. Habermas, in contrast, has consistently argued in favor of maintaining the constitutionally guaranteed rights of asylum seekers and has called for better immigration laws, which would finally recognize that Germany has become an *Einwanderungsland* (immigration country) like the United States.[6] However, such recognition is difficult to achieve, to say the least, as the German national discourse is still based on the assumption of an ethnically homogeneous population.

A third reason why Habermas has been a skeptical observer of German unification is the attempt of the Kohl government to use the fall of the Berlin Wall as an opportunity to 'normalize' the German past. When the reconstitution of the German nation-state is conceived as a return to the German past, for instance to Bismarck's German Empire, the twelve years of National Socialism lose their significance and tend to become a minor flaw within a larger historical tradition. Ever since Bitburg and the Holocaust debate of the mid-1980s, Habermas has consistently challenged this kind of historical revisionism, which ultimately aims to get rid of Germany's moral responsibility for the criminal acts of the Third Reich.[7] Since the unification in 1990, the call for a revision of German history has certainly increased, at least on the conservative side of the debate. Moreover, now the time has come for its application in matters of German foreign policy and cultural self-definition. The reemergence of a conception of Germany as the center of *Mitteleuropa* is only one of a number of symptomatic shifts. For Habermas, this is not merely a matter of geopolitics but a more fundamental question of political and moral grounding. For him the affiliation of the Federal Republic with the West symbolizes the acceptance of liberal democracy that the old Germany had resisted for almost a century.

MORALITY AND POLITICS

For Habermas, the discussion of political issues is inseparable from moral questions. In this respect he has stayed close to a position that he developed in *The Structural Transformation of the Public Sphere* (1962). Harking back to the model of the enlightened public sphere of the eighteenth century, Habermas argued in 1962 that the moral discussion of the Enlightenment, insofar as it was public, prepared the discussion of political emancipation as well. More specifically, he stressed that the public character of the moral discourse also changed the nature of the political discourse. Political decisions and strategies, previously the privilege of the absolutist prince, became, at least in theory, accessible to the public at large. The theoretical locus classicus for this reversal of the relationship between morality and politics is of course Kant's famous essay 'What Is Enlightenment?,' which defined human emancipation as a process carried out through public discussion, which is set up to challenge the tradition. This model, although in Kant's case still operating within the confines of enlightened despotism, undercuts the notion of unquestionable authority and provides a rational procedure for arriving at equitable political decisions.

Habermas's later reformulation of this model in terms of a theory of communicative action is very much in evidence in *The Past as Future* when he discusses the situation of contemporary Germany and the Gulf War. The parameters of these discussions were set by the idea of power politics on the one hand and a utopian conception of the political order on the other. Habermas seeks to locate a middle ground where political conflicts can be addressed rationally within the context of definable norms, which are open to critical scrutiny.

Habermas brings these considerations to bear on the question of German unification as well as the Gulf War. As I pointed out, the German Gulf War debate focused on different issues and was marked by different dividing lines. It is worth noticing that Habermas, in his cautiously worded support for military intervention, emphasizes the legal aspect, especially Saddam Hussein's violation of international law (*Völkerrecht*). That emphasis is clearly directed against two schools of thought in Germany, namely, the traditional Marxist interpretation, which underscored the economic dimension of the conflict, and the conservative reading of the war, which tended to follow Carl Schmitt's argument about the fundamental nature of all political conflicts as friend-foe relationships.

It is not accidental that Habermas's discussion of the Gulf War refers to and makes use of Kant's essay 'On Perpetual Peace.' Habermas specifically argues that the Gulf War cannot be reduced to a raw power struggle between the United States and Saddam Hussein or, more generally speaking, between the industrialized West and a struggling postcolonial Middle East. That is to say, Habermas takes seriously a construction that the Western powers acted on behalf of the United Nations. While Habermas readily admits that the Gulf War cannot be adequately described as a mere police action ordered by the United Nations, his interpretation of the war places in the foreground its normative aspect, a dimension of considerable importance for the future of international relations. Habermas not only underlines the desirability of overcoming traditional power politics but also holds out the realistic possibility of accomplishing a new, morally justified procedure for regulating international conflicts. Such a procedure would require a consistent separation of self-interests and political tasks on the part of the major powers. Yet Habermas clearly stresses the feasibility of legitimate military interventions sanctioned by rules and norms of international law. This principle does not legitimate all available means, however. As Habermas states, 'this question [the legitimacy of extreme means in the Gulf War] can hardly receive an affirmative answer' (15).

Still, Habermas does not shy away from the use of military force, which of course entails inflicting violence against the enemy, as long as it is a strictly regulated use of force where the military means are appropriate for achieving the intended moral and political goals. What is important for Habermas here is the use of procedural legal rationality, since he views these legal norms as grounded in a philosophical discourse dealing with basic principles of human interaction: 'I'm convinced . . . that the basic content of the moral principles embodied in international law is in harmony with the normative substance of the great world-historical prophetic doctrines and metaphysical worldviews' (20–21).

Habermas wants to define the process of German unification in similar ways as a process fraught not only with material problems but also involved in fundamental moral and
ethical questions. Already during the 1980s Habermas tena-
ciously argued against the 'normalization' of the German
past, that is, the erasure of the killing of millions of people
in the name of the German nation during World War II.
Similarly, he has scrutinized German nationalism after the
fall of the Berlin Wall with considerable detachment and
skepticism, since it seems to reflect a mode of thinking that
is not necessarily compatible with the democratic foundations of the Federal Republic. In particular, he wants to
separate national self-interest from the democratic rationality of consensus and dissent – for instance, the difference
between, on the one hand, the interests of German politicians and industrial leaders in German unification and, on
the other, the normative basis required to carry out the as-
similation of the East German population into the Federal
Republic.

As we have seen, Habermas shows no regret for the demise of the GDR, but he is concerned about the future of its
former citizens in the new Federal Republic. This is more
than a matter of lifestyle and private needs; it touches on
the political traditions that are invoked to provide legitimacy to the political institutions. For this reason, Habermas professes uneasiness with the term *die Wende* (the
turning point) for the events of 1989 and prefers to speak of
a revolution (in spite of its lack of planning and decisive
leadership). For the same reason he is also sharply critical
of the mode and the tempo of the unification process,
which was dictated by the Federal Republic rather than the
East German *Volkskammer* (parliament). This criticism

does not question the legitimacy of the process, however; rather, it focuses on the lack of a democratic consensus, the lack of broad popular participation in the process – a political participation that would have expressed itself through the call for a new constitution replacing the interim Basic Law of the old Federal Republic. 'Unification hasn't been understood as a normatively willed act of the citizens of both states, who in political self-awareness decided on a common civil union' (44).

What Habermas seems to fear most about a unification process administered from above is its potential political fallout in the future – namely, the erosion of a democratic political culture as it had developed in West Germany since the late 1960s. He suspects that the newly evoked national identity will fail 'to produce a deep identification with a social order whose universalistic principles anchor a potential for self-criticism and self-transformation' (49). Habermas's critique of German unification, in other words, is primarily concerned about the moral damage done to the civil society and the political culture of Germany. While the East Germans were looking for individual freedom and material improvement, the West Germans were, as Habermas points out, never formally asked to choose between two states and unification. Consequently, the procedure was legitimate (it was ratified both by the *Bundestag* and the *Volkskammer*), but it remained deficient in normative terms.

THE PUBLIC SPHERE

In his discussion of the Gulf War and his treatment of German unification, Habermas emphasizes the link between politics and morality. In both cases that emphasis is grounded in his conception of political practice as working out a consensus (as distinct from compromise) through procedures of communicative interaction.

Ever since his first major book, *The Structural Transformation of the Public Sphere,* Habermas has been a keen and critical observer of Germany's political culture. The reconstitution of a public sphere, which enables the citizens to partake in free political discussion, was and has remained for Habermas a crucial achievement of the young Federal Republic. Habermas has perceived this change as an opening up to the West, bringing about the appropriation of Western models of democracy. That is possibly one of the reasons why Habermas has remained rather cool to the idea of restoring a traditional notion of German nationalism. While in his 1962 study Habermas was mostly interested in analyzing the decline of the public sphere as a result of advanced capitalism and the welfare state, his more recent essays, as well as this interview, stress the specifically German factors of the post-Wall development of the public sphere. The accelerated transformation of the political and cultural climate after 1989 – much faster and more radical than most observers had anticipated – has also affected the character of the public sphere. Whether one has to speak of a structural transformation is at this point an open question. In any case, for Habermas recent events in Germany, including the outbreak of xenophobia, the use of violence against marginal groups, and the belligerent atmosphere of literary debates, suggest a serious setback for democracy and a return of ideas and practices that liberal intellectuals had considered no longer possible.

Habermas's old analysis, which focused on the formalization of the parliament and the pressure of the welfare state in Western democracies, could hardly offer a solution to the new problems. Thus the model of the public sphere had to be reformulated in terms of the relationship between the civil society and the state on the one hand and the economy on the other. As Habermas points out in the introduction to the latest German edition of *Structural Transformation*,[8] the East European discussion of the civil-society model as a critique of state socialism has also influenced the debate about the structure of the public sphere in Western countries such as the Federal Republic. Here we must mention the leftist tradition of the student movement, the peace movement, and the movement of *Bürgerinitiativen* (civil initiatives): they are forms of alternative political practices and examples of democratic participation that transcend the formalism of the political institutions as they functioned in the early years of the Federal Republic. Unlike his conservative opponents and critics, Habermas does not perceive the disturbing changes in Germany as contingent events caused by small groups of youthful offenders; instead, he points to the link between their acts of violence and a publicly sanctioned xenophobic discourse. As Habermas has emphasized in a more recent essay,[9] the real – that is, structural – problem is not the youthful perpetrators of the violence but the state and its police forces, which through their passivity condone acts of violence against foreign minorities. The recent German debate about asylum seekers comes to mind as an example of this dangerous intertwinement of political manipulation by insecure politicians (from the right to the left) and popular sentiment against foreigners.[10] The call for a change of the Basic Law to restrain immigration left the broad public with the impression that foreigners were a potential danger to the welfare of the German people. Habermas has consistently reminded his German audience that these events and the response to them in the mass media has adversely affected the political climate of the Federal Republic.

THE ROLE OF THEORY

In the United States Habermas's reputation is almost exclusively based on his theoretical writings, and especially on his more recent work, published during the 1980s. By contrast, in Germany Habermas is a highly visible public figure, in this respect comparable to Foucault in France. Because of his numerous political interventions, the relationship between theory and practice has been a focus for the discussion of Habermas's work. Of course, that link has always been at the center of the conception of Critical Theory. Max Horkheimer's famous 1937 essay 'Traditional and Critical Theory' underscored the connection as one of the distinctive aspects of a critical approach.[11] And again, in the late 1960s, this link became the focus for the strident debate between the student movement and the older generation of the Frankfurt school.[12] While Habermas at that point cautioned the students against the confusion of symbolic protest and political revolution, he never denied the importance of and the need for political action informed by theory. When one compares his essays from the late 1960s with the last chapter of *The Past as Future,* two things become apparent: first, his later statements are considerably more cautious when they address the nexus of theory and practice; second, and more importantly, the emphasis itself has shifted. Whereas the debate of the 1960s focused on the political application of a theory that was more or less taken for granted, the debate of the 1990s questions the feasibility of and the need for theory.

Habermas suggests that this problematization of ideas and ideological categories does not concern his own theory, which he does not want to be understood as a merely counterfactual conceptual apparatus. Instead, he conceives of theory as a procedural approach to practical questions. Habermas seeks out procedural rationality as a means of dealing with social and political reality. In the process, he redefines classical concepts such as emancipation and enlightenment, which of course played a central role in the work of the first generation of the Frankfurt school and continued to be central to Habermas's early work. Procedural rationality enables processes of communication and interaction that may result in individual emancipation, but it also becomes obvious that Habermas has more or less retreated from an understanding of emancipation that is based on a concept of society as a collective subject (an understanding deeply embedded in the Hegelian Marxist tradition). This redefinition of classical concepts also removes the possibility of or the need for a predetermined goal (of history) and allows for a more positive consideration of political compromise in the political arena of advanced capitalist democracies.

Interestingly enough, Habermas's insistence on the force of normative concepts as inherent in everyday language does not lead him to reject compromise as a means of political consensus formation; rather, it moves him toward a model of decision making in which the pragmatic give-and-take of daily politics is guided by an implicit understanding of moral values that are present even when they are not in the foreground. Clearly, Habermas thereby rejects a reading of his theory of communicative action that stresses the split between an idealized speech situation on the one hand and, on the other hand, the rough-and-tumble of the 'real world' where such normative considerations do not affect the decision-making process. While Michael Haller's questions underscore the contradiction between theory and practice, Habermas upholds the compatibility of our actual linguistic practices and the implied normative element of all linguistic communication. Moreover, turning against Niklas Luhmann and systems theory, Habermas stresses the 'eminent capability and productivity of socially circulating everyday speech' (116).

Still, during the 1980s Habermas has become considerably more restrained in his conceptualization of the theory-practice nexus. Yet unlike the late Adorno, who pointed to the inevitable rupture between philosophy and politics, Habermas means to maintain a (highly mediated) connection between the two realms. Hence he continues to insist on the guiding function of theoretical work for our understanding of and response to social and cultural processes that determine our lifeworld. Thus the role of philosophy appears to be twofold: it reflects, mostly indirectly, the effect of cultural and social institutions, and it engages in a discursive dialogue with its own time. In this definition there is room for a variety of divergent approaches. Habermas's emphasis on the possibility of different and conflicting perspectives, the inclusion of divergent and contradictory theoretical traditions (Luhmann, Jacques Derrida, Foucault) may come as a surprise, since Habermas has tended to demarcate not only the difference between his own position and competing theories but has also tended to stress the greater validity of Critical Theory.

NOTES

1. A representative English selection is to be found in Jürgen Habermas, *The New Conservatism: Cultural Criticism and the Historians' Debate,* ed. and trans. Shierry Weber Nicholsen, (Cambridge, MA: MIT Press, 1989).

2. For an interpretative account of the Historians' Debate see Charles S. Maier, *The Unmasterable Past: History, Holocaust, and German National Identity* (Cambridge, MA: Harvard University Press, 1988).

3. Jürgen Habermas, 'Heinrich Heine and the Role of the Intellectual in Germany,' in *The New Conservatism,* 78.

4. A representative selection of the German post-Wall debate is available in *When the Wall Came Down: Reactions to German Unification,* ed. Harold James and Marla Stone (New York: Routledge, 1992).

5. For details see translator's note 16, p.172.

6. Most recently in his lecture delivered in Paris in January 1993.

7. See for example Jürgen Habermas, 'On the Public Use of History,' in *The New Conservatism,* 229–40.

8. An English version of this introduction can be found in *Habermas and the Public Sphere,* ed. Craig Calhoun (Cambridge, MA: MIT Press, 1992), 421–61, under the title 'Further Reflections on the Public Sphere.'

9. Jürgen Habermas, 'Die zweite Lebenslüge der Bundesrepublik: Wir sind wieder "normal" geworden,' *Die Zeit,* 18 December 1992. For details see also translator's note 18, p.178 (The Asylum Debate).

10. See for instance Gisela Dachs, '"Den Haß krieg ich nicht mehr los,"' *Die Zeit,* 8 January 1993.

11. Max Horkheimer, 'Traditional and Critical Theory,' in *Critical Theory: Selected Essays* (New York: Seabury Press, n.d.), 188–243.

12. See the collection of essays in the volume *Die Linke antwortet Jürgen Habermas* (Frankfurt am Main: Europäische Verlagsanstalt, 1968), which focuses on Habermas's supposed lack of revolutionary radicalism.

THE PAST AS FUTURE

Preface by Michael Haller

With the collapse of state socialism in Eastern Europe, with the Iraquis in Kuwait and Americans in the Persian Gulf, and with the politics of self-interest in Bonn and the terrific social need of those in the East who longed for West German conditions, a new obscurity – to borrow a title from Jürgen Habermas[1] – has arisen in our world. And with this new obscurity grows the need for new answers and new interpretations.

Generating new explanations to a changing social and political world is the idea behind this book, which seeks to place contemporary problems and political events in the clarifying light of Habermasian analysis.

Initially scheduled for the summer of 1990, my interview with Jürgen Habermas was ultimately conducted by correspondence: I began it toward the close of that year with a number of questions concerning the Germans in Europe; it continued in February 1991 with reflections on the crisis in the Middle East, and concluded in March 1991 with some broader questions concerning Jürgen Habermas's political thought.

The written form of the interview will not, of course, permit the kind of spontaneity and conversational give-and-take that one expects from spoken interviews. But it compensates the reader with the clarity of its construction and the succinctness of its form.

In this interview, my questions and Jürgen Habermas's answers group themselves according to a progression dictated by the course of events themselves: from the historical flash point of the Persian Gulf, we moved to the situation of Germany and its intellectuals, then on to Europe as a whole, and finally, to questions on the validity of Habermasian theory in an epoch tormented by anxiety about its own future.

Times such as these, when new and unsettling events demand a continuous examination of one's own judgments, make up-to-date interviews very perishable. During the course of our interview Jürgen Habermas has worried about this – unnecessarily, as it turns out, for his comments touch on questions and problems that extend far beyond the contemporary events themselves, opening up new perspectives and new possibilities for dialogue, creating impetus for new analyses in a debate that is only now beginning: the debate on what will become of Eastern and Western Europe. I thank Jürgen Habermas for the care he took, despite the rapid whirl of events in the first months of 1991, to carry out this interview with me to its end.

Prologue

MICHAEL HALLER: *At the beginning of the decade, we are preoccupied – and threatened – by two dramatic events.*

The first is the lightning-fast collapse of real, existing socialism in Eastern Europe, a collapse that drove the Soviet Union to the brink of civil war, but that also bestowed on us Germans the unification of the two Germanies on 3 October 1990 – a historical event with wide-reaching consequences not just for us but for the political fabric of Europe as a whole.

The second event emerged with Iraq's annexation of Kuwait in August 1990. This act provoked an ultimatum from the United Nations Security Council. The result, on 16 January 1991, was a Washington-led allied attack on Iraq – a six-week war with clear consequences not just for the people of the Middle East but also for relations between the industrialized nations and the Third World.

The Gulf War: Catalyst for a
New German Normalcy?

MICHAEL HALLER: *I'd like to begin this written interview with the events in the Persian Gulf, which have sparked vigorous debates around the globe. Many people perceived the Gulf War as a relapse into sheer barbarism, a reversion that one would scarcely have thought possible any longer. Was it? Or, on the contrary, can it be understood as the* ultima ratio *for preventing even worse barbarism?*

» «

JÜRGEN HABERMAS: That was *the* most emotionally charged, intellectually explosive question in January and February 1991. The intensity of this heated debate is itself a phenomenon worthy of investigation. Why did the Gulf War set loose this wave of emotions and this flood of arguments? There have been hundreds of wars since 1945, some with far more victims, but many of these never even came to the attention of the First World. Of course, this time the conflict involved the oil wells of the Middle East, which are crucial for the industrial production of Western nations, Japan, and elsewhere. But this fact doesn't really explain the public turbulence. One could also say that the wars of a superpower always have a global significance, as it were. But then the reactions to the wars in Korea and Vietnam should have been similar. The intervention in Vietnam was, in fact, a conflict that played itself out before the eyes of a public sphere in the strictest sense. But this time, the crisis didn't arise from a struggle for national liberation as a consequence of decolonialization. It's far more accurate to say

5

that two factors came together that, in conjunction, served to transform the *mode of perception* of the events of the war: the demonstrative rationality of the military planning, and the unparalleled presence of the media.

Because the traumatic failure in Vietnam was not to repeat itself, and because, this time, the 'home front' was to remain stable, the general staff set out with cold calculation to keep everything under control – an operation that was in turn supposed to be universally observable. What had traditionally been experienced as the blind intrusion of destiny, as the sheer source of contingency itself – war – thus was transformed into a kind of 'staged' reality, the enactment of a risk-free, technically hyperefficient, 'clean' commando operation carried out with speed and precision, and with minuscule casualties for one's own side. The press briefings were also under strict control, becoming in effect part of the prosecution of the war, a war that, with its technical simulations, seemed to blend into the television screen itself. It's often been said that the blurred reality of suffering imbued the whole business with an artificial character. The 'staged' war invited comparisons with video games, with the maddeningly irresistible playback of an electronic program. And contrary to expectations, reality never did step forth once the veil of censorship was lifted. To this day the victims remain shadow figures; we can only speculate whether there were a hundred thousand, two hundred thousand, or more. I read one single report of the horrors on the escape road to Basra in the hours before the delayed cease-fire. This tiny piece of authenticity from the pen of an English reporter had nearly the effect of an account of the Thirty Years' War.

Of course, censorship had unforseen consequences as

well. We outside observers were all too aware that a good portion of the reality – in fact, the warlike dimension of the war – was being withheld, and this awareness may have stimulated our own powers of imagination. Reports of the Scud missile attacks on Tel Aviv, or the two thousand sorties on Baghdad in a single day, often reminded me of the aerial bombardments of World War II, of our own destroyed cities. The censor's black patch on the TV screen set one's own imagination in motion. And it directed the gaze of the frustrated observer onto the medium itself. The withheld illumination of this negativity raised tensions, brought the power of the media out into the open, and made sensible the eternal present of an omnipresent, ever-vigilant medium. In short, the constructedness, the very artificiality of the events, as well as the global simultaneity of event, report, and perception, determined our own perceptions of what happened. What drove past us were the slow-motion tank treads of a high-tech war machine – aseptic, purified of any fateful character, lifted out of the horizon of human experience and suffering, sprinkled with a few dashes of 'human touch.' This wasn't just an alienated reality. It was as if the changed mode of perception itself had created an alternative reality. The disproportion of military forces had the further effect of suggesting that war – the essence of contingency – was in fact something within our own power of control.

This is a notion that could have dangerous long-term effects. It counteracts anxieties that indeed were far from unjustified – the fear that the next Scud rocket might carry a chemical warhead, that Saddam could make good on his threat to retaliate with biological weapons or with acts of biological terrorism, or the fear that nuclear weapons could ultimately be used. The demon of nuclear, biological, and chemical weapons was the shadow lurking behind the flaming oil wells. The ecological dimension of the war was new. But it's most accurate to say that the truly new quality of the events was brought out by the contrast between the palpably increasing uncontrollability of the enormous risks inherent in advanced technology, on the one hand, and on the other, that methodicalness and effectiveness with which the war was staged. A power that threatened to blow every dimension of the lifeworld to pieces appeared to be reassuringly drawn back into the lifeworld's horizon. The reversion to barbarism that you spoke of is perhaps too old-fashioned a description for what we watched through the lenses of CNN. The more stylized and fragmented the perception of such an elusive event was, the more our moral feelings could be hijacked, and the more our imagination could be laid claim to by interpretations – interpretations that extend to the political dimensions of the Gulf War.

»«

What do you mean by the 'political dimensions' of the Gulf War?

»«

From the start, our perceptions have been shaped, even interpreted, through specific categorizations and more or less obvious sorts of analyses. Everyone's arguing, and everyone is at least partly right. The vehemence and the one-sidedness of many of the participants can also be explained by the failure of many of the discussions to distinguish clearly between four different aspects of the war.

I've already mentioned the first of these dimensions: the obvious element of power politics. Naturally, the industrialized nations were terrified of losing control of their sup-

8

ply of crude oil, an essential energy source. Second, the memory of the colonial past in the Middle East cast the conflict in the form of a struggle between the culture of the Christian West, dominating world markets with its technological superiority, and the Arab world. For us too, the global process of decolonialization after the end of World War II had sharpened a certain sensitivity for the experiences of culturally imperiled and fragmented peoples. We've learned that the contradictions of religious socialization can cause deeper fractures than differences in modes of production or class distinctions. A third dimension of the war emerged with Saddam Hussein's threat to use nuclear, biological, or chemical weapons against Israel: the smoldering Palestinian conflict. On psychohistorical grounds alone, gas warfare represented an intolerable threat for Israel, which this time found itself obliged to remain passive. Never before had its very existence been put in question in this way. The obscene connection between the German export of technology into Iraq and Scud rockets, possibly armed with chemical warheads and aimed at Israel, was a particular challenge for the political morality of Germans. Micha Brumlek spoke of a 'litmus test.'[1] The fourth dimension of the war, and one that actually augurs well for the future, was the role of the United Nations in carrying out a global domestic policy [*Weltinnenpolitik*], the authorization – certainly with many conditions attached – for the deployment of military forces.

The implications of the Gulf War for the future status of international law shouldn't be lightly set aside – the inclination of all our *Realpolitiker,* who, whether equipped with their bookbag Marx or bookbag Carl Schmitt, have acquired an a priori certainty that ideas will prostrate themselves before interests every time. In the context of a global society characterized by extreme disproportions in the distribution of opportunity, I don't regard this attitude as particularly realistic. In fact, the dramatic North-South and East-West distinctions in the division of power and prosperity render irrational threats and extortions with nuclear, biological, or chemical weapons, as well as the self-destructive threat of ecological terrorism, increasingly likelier. It would therefore be a reasonable policy to strengthen the authority of the UN sufficiently for the resolutions of the world community to be enforced, if necessary by military means. Chapter 7 of the UN charter already provides for such operations, which are required to take place under the supervision of the UN itself. Now that the Cold War is over, we ought to build up the UN and create an executive force that will be able effectively to exhaust all the legally provided possibilities.

» «

Many UN observers might well object that your call for an executive force is based on an overestimation of the UN. Isn't the United Nations itself dependent on the international constellations of political power within the Security Council?

» «

Please don't confuse this with a call for setting up a world government or – what is truly utopian – a monopoly of power by the UN. In his essay 'On Perpetual Peace,' Kant also rejected a world government and instead called for a 'federation of free states.' The institution of the UN Security Council originated from the need to establish a basis for the UN with the cooperation of interconnected world powers. Without their willingness to cooperate, an international system would remain just as powerless as the UN has been up until now. A peaceful world order would be possible only on the premise that internal factors within the powerful industrialized nations render them in less and less of a position to act externally as belligerent states. Kant maintained that only those states that had achieved an internal republican constitution could band together into a federative order of peace. We too can only hope that the populations of the world's social-welfare democracies gradually develop into liberal political cultures, that they grow accustomed to institutions of freedom and develop majorities with pacifistic mentalities, so that they can no longer be mobilized for wars in the classical sense. Despite the regression into the nationalistic atmosphere of the nineteenth century that we are now observing, long-term trends point in this direction.

When regarded from this perspective, the Gulf War was at best a kind of hybrid. It wasn't carried out under the command of the United Nations; the nations that actually conducted the war weren't even accountable to the UN. And yet the Allies claimed the legitimation of the UN until the end. In theory, they acted as deputies of the world organization. That's better than nothing. It's becoming evident that the enforcement of international law has to be carried out by an organized cooperation of the international community, and not by some utopian (in the worst sense of the word) world government. But this also makes it at least conceivable that the end of the bipolar world order could be the opportunity for a *new* beginning. In hindsight, at least, we have to try to make the best of the Gulf War – the best not only for the Middle East but for the order of international relations as such. This is how I take the most recent remarks of the *Bundespräsident*. With a view to the future, the skeptical reference to praxis *up to the present* loses its convincing power. It's true that, apart from the Korean War (which itself appears as a very dubious precedent when looked at clearly), Western nations have never militarily intervened in cases where the resolutions of the UN have been simply ignored by the governments in question. But the bankruptcy of state socialism has created a new situation. For the first time, the two superpowers acted as one. For the first time, the United States and its allies were offered the objective possibility of temporarily assuming the (presumably neutral) role of police force to the United Nations – a force that is still lacking to this day – to enforce the principles of international law in the defense of what was collectively acknowledged as the injured rights of the Kuwaitis. Nobody can seriously doubt that Iraq's annexation of Kuwait and its announcement of its intention to open a war with Israel, even a war with nuclear, biological, or chemical weapons, constituted an injury to international law.

» «

But the Gulf War, as it was waged between 16 January and 3 March 1991, was hardly a UN police action.

» «

Yes, the claim to the legitimacy of the UN served largely as a pretext. But it illuminates a dimension of the war that one ought to bear in mind, particularly with a view to the *future* of international politics. One can at least *appeal* to the norms that the superpowers invoked. As I said, the war was at best a kind of hybrid. It was never a police action, and bit by bit it devolved into the unchecked brutality of a very normal war. In fact, the UN was criticized for allowing itself to become a tool of the United States. But even these objections appeal to the criteria of international law and don't refute them easily. A normative assessment of the war would have to take into account above all the restrictions imposed by the legitimation of the UN. That's true not only for the military objectives. Above all, the concessions to the UN would have required the superpowers to separate their role as agents of the international community from their own interests, which, as industrialized Western countries, they naturally also have. It would have been absolutely necessary to avoid three different confusions: First, the intervention was to have remained recognizable worldwide as a police action; it would, so to speak, not be waged as a normal war. Second, there was to be no suspicion that the first priority of the West was securing its own access to its energy source – no blood for oil. Finally, care was to be taken that the war not be perceived as a conflict between the West and the Arab world.

» «

A lot of slogans – many naïve, some surely stupid – were in circulation during the opening phase of the Gulf War. But there was also a number of powerful and thought-provoking arguments against the war. Let me offer the following two: Not only did the United States and the secretary general of the United Nations fail to bring about an end of hostilities through negotiations, but they failed even to make a serious attempt to do so. Instead, they inflated numbers to dramatize Saddam Hussein's military threat and then confronted him with an ultimatum for an immediate and unconditional withdrawal from Kuwait that was bound to be unacceptable for an Arab leader to swallow. Second, it can be argued that the Western world failed to summon the Israeli government to participate in a Mideast peace conference before time ran out and the ultima-

tum went into effect. A peace conference would have offered a real chance for a solution to the crisis in the Middle East, linked as it is to the fate of the Palestinians. According to this second argument, the Gulf War served to mask this failure and thus has rendered the Western nations even more untrustworthy in the eyes of many Arabs than they were already.

» «

You're quite right. The conditions that you name – the exhaustion of all possibilities for negotiation, an ethically responsible calculation of the possible consequences of the war, and the appropriateness of the military means to be employed – were supposed to be fulfilled before the Allies made use of their UN authorization and launched an attack on Iraq. It's a bit academic to subject an event of such brutality to a pedantically normative assessment after the fact. The arguments, and the points of disagreement, have been discussed the world over: the possibility that a longer embargo would have worked, the difficulties of intercultural understanding, the question of whether a settlement that includes the Palestinians is really easier now than it was before, and so on. We're not going to be able to contribute anything new to this.

» «

A third objection to the Gulf War goes something like this: Perhaps the military action by the UN was in fact necessary. But the manner in which the United States directed the air war – area bombardment, near-total destruction of several cities such as Basra, a horribly high number of victims among the Iraqi civilian population, and above all the destruction of the natural environment – transformed a war of liberation for Kuwait into a war of destruction against the state of Iraq. On these grounds the Gulf War flagrantly violated the basic prin-

*ciple of appropriate means in international law: the military
objective, the liberation of Kuwait, stands in no proper proportion to this irreparable destruction. Thus the war cannot be
justified according to the principles of international law. In
short: even according to the norms imposed by Western civilization, the West countered the injustices of Saddam Hussein
with new injustices of its own. Do you regard objections of this
kind to be justified?*

» «

The question of the appropriateness of a military strategy
that included area bombardment and that produced hundreds of thousands killed and wounded, huge streams of
refugees, enormous destruction of the civilian infrastructure, long-term ecological damage, and persistent catastrophic conditions in both Iraq and Kuwait – this question
can hardly receive an affirmative answer. But I think that, at
least in regard to Israel – that is, the nightmare scenario of
an Israel encircled by the entire Arab world and threatened
with the most horrific kinds of weapons – the authorization
for military sanctions against Iraq was justified. Even if all
the conditions that were supposed to have been fulfilled for
this authorization to be used had actually been met, we
need to bear in mind that, from a moral and a legal stand-
point, the war was justified solely in the form of a police
action, one that was to take careful aim in employing precisely those means that would produce compliance with
the resolutions of the international community. Hindsight
is always 20–20 – that's part of the essence of historical
events.

» «

*Various observers of the Middle East scene said quite early
that Saddam Hussein was an Arab version of Hitler, and that*

he was determined to annihilate anyone and anything that
stood in the way of his own grandiose fantasies. In a Spiegel
essay from the third week of the war, Hans-Magnus Enzen-
berger[2] *wrote that, like Hitler, Hussein was the personified 'foe*
of humanity,' whose objective was the extinction of the human
race – the final solution, a campaign of extermination that
placed all the powers of human passions, dammed-up resent-
ments, and religious faith in its service. 'All attempts to inter-
pret him ideologically, or even to refute him' must therefore
fail: 'His project is carried out through obsessions, not ideas'
(Der Spiegel 6 [1991]). Are we really talking about a threat to
the human race, a genocidal psychopath who began his insane
rampage with his attack on Iran, and who was only finally
stopped in the spring of 1991?

» «

You don't give up easily, do you? I've long regarded Enzenberger as the most brilliant – and cleverest – intellectual
figure of my generation. But he doesn't distinguish himself
with his political acuity. He's an intellectual who's trying to
see how far he can run with a crazy hypothesis. On the one
side, the German middle classes who never managed to
cozy up to the Republic after Versailles; on the other side,
the Iraqi people, bled white by an eight-year war with Iran;
nationalistic German prejudices here, Shiite fundamentalism there – but where is the common historical denominator for the atavism of humiliated populations, from whose
death wish dictatorships are supposed to be born? Before
this anthropologizing gaze, in the flight into subhistory,
all substantial distinctions dissolve. What's more, we've
learned from the story of Hitler historiography that the demonization of the great Führer personality always distorts
our view of historical facts. Enzenberger needs to be taken

seriously, not as a historian or political analyst, but as a seismograph. He's got his nose in the wind. He had only recently lent his pen to the muddled indifference of libertarianism and the praise of mediocrity. If he's now turned to hunting down arguments for the war party, this may be a sign of a sea change in attitudes, perhaps a transition from the French to the German postmodern: from Lyotard to Bohrer?[3]

The counterpiece to the muttering of the political class over the new international responsibility and the rediscovered normalcy of Greater Germany finds its expression in the feuilleton of the *Frankfurter Allgemeine Zeitung*. The editor's front-page complaint about the Germans' flight from politics and their collective failure before the existential seriousness of the war is, in the feuilleton, pushed to a sophisticated literary plateau. Thus Kleist is cited on the question of whether a country wholly devoid of a sense of political tragedy can survive. The emphasis on the joys of national unity pales in the gray shadows of the jobless masses; in the aesthetic semblance of electronically controlled storms of steel, it now takes on a new coloring: 'Reunification has given the nation back the vocabulary of state symbolism. Now would have been the time for it to speak in this language for the first time. Instead it remained mute, and now must pay for it' (*Frankfurter Allgemeine Zeitung*, 18 February 1991). Now the heros, the hardened desert foxes, will once again confront the shopkeepers, the meekest civilians who would rather pay than die. Instead of putting their own necks out, the postwar Germans celebrate their own whining faintheartedness. If one were to take the tenor of this kind of complaint seriously, we'd be in for a reprise of the ideas of 1914, dolled up in early Romanticism.

I have to confess that the one single good news story during this interminable TV coverage between 6 and 9 A.M. was a report on the military chaplains at the German air base in Turkey. The base commander refused to allow the camera crews to film the service because the troops couldn't keep from crying. Sensitivity isn't Romanticism's worst legacy.

» «

We'll return later to the special role of Germany. Let me come back for a moment to the conflict in the Middle East. It's clear that Saddam Hussein found such broad support in the Arab world, indeed the Third World as a whole, because he dared to stand up to the self-righteousness and arrogance of the West. 'He showed us the righteous path,' a Sudanese government spokesman said after the third week of the war. Seen in this way, the Western world, with its Eurocentric politics of igno-rance, sowed a wind it's now reaping as a whirlwind. What is your judgment of our own share in the guilt?

» «

Whatever Saddam Hussein's fate will be after the ruthless civil war that he is now waging against the Kurds and Shiites, he will have lost his aura and will be reduced to the level of one of many national potentates scrabbling for ad-vantage in the fragmented Arab region. This doesn't get rid of the phenomenon that you correctly refer to – the under-standable disposition of the masses to win back for their Islamic world a measure of self-respect against a Western world that is still perceived as colonialist. This is also what makes Israel's position – as long as it is still obliged to act as an outpost of the Western world – so precarious. One of the possible unintended consequences of the war could be the strengthening of Iran and the spread of Islamic fundamentalism. If religious fundamentalism is understood as a reaction against the destructive and socially fragmenting aspects of social modernization, then the historical burden of responsibility of Western imperialism is undeniable. Indeed, modernization stood and still stands under the sign of a capitalism that is far more than just an economic form. But material poverty and political oppression are *also* the responsibility of the indigenous elites, whether they react in a totalitarian manner or not, whether they are corrupted or not – all have become accomplices. The more complex such dependencies become, the sharper our awareness is of cultural conflicts that still permit univocal inside-outside polarizations – and the more they will be exploited politically.

The Arab world is built on one of the world's oldest high cultures. Moreover, in Islam the Arab world can call upon a religious tradition that is an equal to Christianity. The West has a great deal to learn about the subtle questions of intercultural understanding between regions and peoples. But there are also encouraging signs. Over the past few decades, the relatively heavy immigration process has not only set off the familiar xenophobic reactions in Western societies but has also brought to light the problems of the coexistence – under equal rights – of different cultural ways of life. The United States was a multiethnic society from its very inception. But even here the scales have shifted dramatically in favor of the minorities: the last census shows that a quarter of the population is of non-European ancestry. That corresponds to the proportion of foreigners in a large German city such as Frankfurt. The Shiite revolution in Iran, the Salman Rushdie affair and its consequences, and now the Gulf War and nationalist conflicts in Eastern

Europe have also reminded us in the secularized West of the explosiveness and the continuing significance of religiously rooted national conflicts. This grants a remarkable contemporary relevance not just to Kant's idea of perpetual peace but also to Lessing's theme of reconciliation between world religions.

And here we encounter one of the very few philosophical problems with an immediate political relevance. Are the principles of international law so intertwined with the standards of Western rationality – a rationality built in, as it were, to Western culture – that such principles are of no use for the nonpartisan adjudication of international conflicts? For example, does the claim to universality that we connect with the concept of human rights simply conceal an especially subtle and deceitful instrument of domination of one culture over another – as in the slogan 'Whoever speaks of "humanity" is a liar'? Or is it the case that universal world religions *converge* in some core condition of moral intuition according to their own claims, a core that we interpret as equal respect for all, equal respect for the need to promote the integrity of each individual person, and for the damageable intersubjectivity of all forms of human existence? Is there not, as my colleague John Rawls maintains, an 'overlapping consensus' within world perspectives and religious interpretations of deep moral feelings and elementary experiences of communicative interaction? Is this a consensus on which the world community could support the norms of a peaceful coexistence? The philosophical discussion on these topics is in a state of flux. But I'm convinced that Rawls is right, that the basic content of the moral principles embodied in international law is in harmony with the normative substance of the great world-historical prophetic doctrines and metaphysical world-views.

Of course, the followers of these doctrines and world-views ought not to remain closed off from one another in sectarian isolation. They must discursively engage themselves – not only with each other, but with the intellectual content of European modernity as well. To this extent they must take a reflective step beyond the universe of their own beliefs. In this sense, today's decisive controversies are taking place within traditions themselves, within Islam, but also within Christianity; between the tide of fundamentalism and those who are determined to reflect on the pluralistic challenge of modern society. Openness to the world, however, mustn't lead to the apathy of a shopworn liberalism, as the example of Johann Baptist Metz's opposition to the Eurocentrism of the Catholic church illustrates. A second fault line of conflict runs through secular postmetaphysical thinking itself. Here the counterpart to religious fundamentalism forms the skepticism of a self-destructive critique of reason, one that senses behind every universal validity claim the dogmatic will to domination of a cunningly concealed particularism. Ever since the influential work of Carl Schmitt, this antihumanistic form of thought has stamped itself on the intellectuals of the right, and unfortunately of the left as well, particularly here in Germany. Intellectuals of this stripe would like to banish arguments grounded in categories of morality and international law from politics altogether, because they can recognize such arguments only as the rationalistic masquerade of sheer, existential self-assertion. After the Gulf War, we've witnessed a rebirth of this false concretism of the neoconservative celebration of aestheticized power, haloed greatness, and political charisma.

»«

But there's also such a thing as false universalism. In view of a world rapidly drifting into new spheres of interest, of growing disparities of power and prosperity between East and West, North and South, how could the term 'global domestic policy' be given something like a concrete content?

»«

The idea of a 'global domestic policy' – I believe the term was coined by Carl Friedrich von Weisäcker[4] – is in fact connected with the Kantian vision of a cosmopolitan state, one that our Schmittians ridicule as mere 'good intention.' Surely, everyone today is in agreement that the idea of a just and peaceful cosmopolitan order lacks any historical and philosophical support. But what other choice do we have, besides at least striving for its realization?

We've discussed the fact that the United States and its allies appealed to the legitimation of the UN. This is a fact. The institutions of the UN, and the basic principles of international law expressed in the UN charter, embody what Hegel would have called a piece of 'existential reason' – a small portion of the idea that Kant had already clearly formulated two hundred years ago. It's no longer merely a vague ideal. There are certain demands that derive from this claim to legitimation. These are only demands, of course. But insofar as such demands are made forcefully, and, what is more important, to the extent that these demands become politically convincing, they are also now a piece of reality. I'm speaking now of normative implications.

The Western powers must get clear on the duties and

responsibilities that they implicitly assume when they make use of this legitimation. For example – and this would already in itself imply a radical transformation of Western politics – they would have to put a stop to the trafficking in death by radically curtailing arms exports from manufacturing countries. So far, the political will for this has been lacking. Further, the Western powers would have to be prepared to strengthen the executive force of the UN and to move ahead with the institutionalization of a peaceful world order equipped with a neutral armed force capable of enforcing UN resolutions. And still further, they would have to take far more seriously their responsibility for the establishment of a just world economy – for a fairer distribution of opportunity on a shrinking planet. Finally, the Western powers would have to overcome the imperialistic attitude that the West has nothing to learn from other cultures and move toward a symmetrical process of cross-cultural understanding.

Now, you'll immediately object that these are precisely the kind of universalistic slogans that have served simply to cover over the business of politics as usual. That's not entirely false, but neither is it entirely true. Each of these normative demands can be matched up with real and increasingly unavoidable problems; if left unresolved, those problems will lead to consequences that the West will feel as sanctions.

We're talking about the Gulf War, a war that was virtually universally perceived as the continuation, by atavistic means, of a ruinously unsuccessful politics. If such things aren't simply to repeat themselves, then our efforts have to go into dismantling the category of war – not into the new category of 'executive actions,' as Horst-Eberhard Richter

has named the Gulf War, but rather reconfigured as interventions of a military force under the command of the UN.
Of course, even this is only treating symptoms unless it can
also simultaneously lead to a revisioning of the category of
foreign policy as a multilaterally coordinated world domestic policy. But for this too there are at least institutional nu-
clei, on the model of international organizations or standing conferences.

»«

*Let's now focus on the role of the Germans. Only a few months
before the beginning of the Gulf War, the superpowers had allowed the unification of the two German states, and in so doing
may well have overseen the birth of a new superpower. In the
past the superpowers had always welcomed Germany's reluctance to take on any pivotal position in world politics. But now
Germany is being heavily criticized for its failure to pitch in
politically or militarily to the allied war effort in the Persian
Gulf. It looks as if the ward is now to become the warden. Is
that the case?*

»«

That's a riddle for the mass psychologists. Particularly for
Germany's European neighbors, the criticisms of the crafty
Germans and their international arms business (a business
that others have indeed pursued in the same style, and
often on a larger scale) gave vent to a lot of very ambivalent
feelings – feelings that had been bottled up during the star-
tling unification process and Germany's graduation to
America's 'partner in leadership.' But sending draftees to
the Persian Gulf – instead of professional soldiers recruited
from the underclasses, along with their career officers – is
another matter altogether. I don't want to speculate any further on that.

Here at home, our reactions to the criticism of our allies has given rise to a rather peculiar situation. The right pins the blame for such criticism squarely on its own government, and warns of a new German special path – not so much because they fear it, but because, with the misleading notion of a German 'normalcy' to be rewon, they see a chance of finally crossing that finish line that had always been out of their reach. One sees this most recently in the Historians' Debate.[5]

I won't deny that the government made mistakes. It was too preoccupied with other things – for example, with the problem of finding a way out of the self-imposed case of 'Steuerlüge'[6] – to carry out a *timely* analysis of the international situation. Even during the months when the time period of the ultimatum was ticking by, the government wasn't able to get clear on what its own position should be regarding an imminent military operation in the gulf. If it weren't for this failure, the government could well have had some influence on the adherence to the conditions for a military action licensed by the UN. And so they in effect reacted incoherently to a fait accompli – with a rash of arms shipments and some shamefaced checks, written with a guilty conscience. The Israeli writer David Grossman[7] has said that Israel shouldn't accept this money – 'because it smells of bribery.' But whatever our government did wrong, at least its policy of refusing to send German Tornados to attack Baghdad was, God knows, no mistake. In memory of the global ambitions of a German *Reich* that plunged Europe into two world wars, the policy was also the expression of a historically well-grounded inhibition. I can understand Yorim Kaniuk[8] when he appeals to us Germans, especially to those of us who protested against the war, to practice solidarity with the endangered state of Israel; to place ourselves empathetically in the position of Israelis who night after night had to pull on gas masks and run for cover in sealed rooms. Even if Günter Grass was the false addressee, Kaniuk was right to invoke the special responsibility of the Germans for the existence and the protection of his vulnerable country. I'm not implying that this kind of desperate dialogue comes down to Israelis playing with the guilty consciences of Germans, as my friend Ernst Tugendhat[9] has objected. It's a matter of moral self-understanding, of remaining alert to the sensibility for incomparable injuries that are bequeathed to the next generation, and the one after that. And this means simply that these special duties ought to remain recognizable in the rational foundation of sober political judgments. But the distorted echo that this and similar appeals find around here is something quite different. The well-known apologists for tough-mindedness now feel themselves encouraged to brand as 'flight from political responsibility' a mentality of caution and restraint that had been carefully built up over decades. But that is the wrong answer. It took long enough for postwar Germany to draw the rational conclusions from the catastrophic end of its own 'special path' – or its own 'special consciousness,' insofar as it split itself off from the traditions of Western civilization. Denouncing these very conclusions as just so many symptoms of a new 'special consciousness' is not merely a twisting of words but a grotesque distortion of historical facts.

»«

A lot has been written on the special consciousness and the special path of Germans, as well as on the question of a new normalcy as a consequence of German unification. But a great

*many people, above all those in the peace movement, insist
that the National Socialist past demands a special role for the
new Germany in only one respect: to stand for a politics of
radical pacifism, notwithstanding all its ties to the West and its
part in the process of (West) European integration. Or are such
demands simply naïve?*

» «

That's a central question, but also a very touchy one. It's so
delicate because a wrongly intoned answer leads into the
trap of negative nationalism, which indeed many people
accuse us of. If after forty-five years the citizens of the Federal Republic are really to have learned something from the
catastrophic mistakes of their fathers and grandfathers –
and we can only hope for this with bated breath – then they
would have made undeserved use of opportunities that
themselves are connected with catastrophes and defeats. In
1988, when I traveled to Moscow for the first time, I was
surprised by the melancholy remark of a Russian colleague:
we, the Germans, were able to learn from the war we lost,
while they, the victors, had somehow been crippled by the
drearily ritualized celebration of the Great War for the Fatherland. This has its trivial side as well. After the unconditional surrender, for example, it wasn't especially hard for
us to refrain from the manufacture of nuclear, biological,
and chemical weapons. After an insane overburdening of
national consciousness, it wasn't hard for Germany to pur-
sue a pacifistic, unobtrusive foreign policy. And without a
form of sovereignty grounded in the categories of international law – which Germany got back only a few days ago –
we also had nothing that we had to give up in favor of European unity, which we therefore pursued all the more ener-
getically. In the end, we really only profited from it.

But you're getting at something else with your reference to the National Socialist past. You mean the question that my friend and Frankfurt colleague Karl-Otto Apel treated in a lecture entitled 'Back to Normalcy? or, Could the National Catastrophe Have Taught Us Something Special?'[10] His answer to this question heads in the direction that you mention. After Hitler and Auschwitz, the Germans have every reason for being particularly sensitive to universalism; that is, for the indivisibility of internationally recognized human rights and for a civilized mode of human interaction. One can take up and reflectively deal with specifically German experiences without ascribing a 'special role' to one's self. At a recent conference in Prague, the Czech historian Jan Kren said that 'management of the past' in the Federal Republic has been one of the 'greatest achievements' of the century. Maybe this is something that *someone else* can say. But the moment we were to compliment ourselves in this way, such a claim – which in any case was meant more evocatively than descriptively – would be rendered null and void. In fact, this kind of claim means only this: following the break in civilization from which the Federal Republic emerged, the situation was so utterly abnormal that it was only the painful avoidance of a purely self-deceptive consciousness of 'normalcy' that allowed the rebirth of halfway normal conditions in this country. First cultivated in the Adenauer years, the feel for this *dialectic of normalization* is now on the wane – in fact, it's being actively discredited.

The past few weeks have seen a discussion over a change in the Basic Law [*Grundgesetz*] that would make possible the deployment of the German army [*Bundeswehr*] outside of NATO territory. It's thus a discussion of three different options: the participation of the German army in logistical and peacekeeping missions of the United Nations, carried out by the 'Blue Helmets,' isn't at issue. The controversy surrounds another, broader kind of engagement. Should the German army be included in an (as yet nonexistent) UN military force, to be used in police actions in cases of injuries to human rights? Or should they also be able to take part in allied military ventures, as in the case of the Gulf War – that is, in military actions by states that simply borrow the legitimation of the UN? This third option is supposedly made palatable by the pledge that a German involvement outside the authority of NATO would be possible only in the framework of a reactivated West European Union (WEU).[11] The debate is couched in highly technical arguments. But it still serves to illuminate the emerging ideological fronts.

The wish for newly expanded possibilities for worldwide military engagement independent of the UN is justified by the need to depart from the dominant politics of 'Genscherism'[12] and thus also from the 'encumbrances' of the postwar period. So far, the backers of an undialectical 'return to normalcy' haven't been successful in bringing it off. But now they see a window of opportunity for *reversing* a transformation of mentality that took place over the last several decades, and for launching Greater Germany on the course toward a 'normalization' that will finally free us of the trauma of mass crimes and give us back our national innocence. The Gulf War serves as a catalyst for this reversal. Of course, this phenomenon is explicable only from the context of a German special consciousness – a consciousness that is now being cheerfully tapped once again. Let me expand on this, with the help of a commentary I find in one of our cultural journals.

The fusion of motives at work is familiar from the days of the *Tatkreise* at the end of the Weimar Republic.[13] First, the ridicule of the abstract universalism of a standard of human morality. The 'terms borrowed from UN-speak, like "peace-keeping unity"' constitute the 'semantically formless gestures of an ideological phraseology,' since 'universalistic categories conceal a vacuum of practical ethics.' In this fashion, stripping away the veil of humanistic nonsense from the 'principle of German reason of state' leads the way back to its political heart: the existential face-to-face of friend and foe. 'The allied troops now, or German units in the future, are war-waging, not peacekeeping: even if they are accompanied by some mission of the UN, they are defending the essential interests of the West against essential interests of the Arab masses and their various dictators.' The war thus lays bare the essence of the political: the life-and-death struggle. Hence the satisfaction over the fact that 'the nonapocalyptic war is thinkable, and thus once again becomes a political tool.' On the means-ends rationality of war making, however, the author has nothing to say. His understanding of the political sustains itself far more from an aestheticization of war. The Anglo-Americans, here described as the 'masters of twentieth-century history,' receive the dubious compliment of having 'dealt self-consciously with the nightmare scenario,' supposedly empowering them to 'obliterate Dresden and Hiroshima almost without moral scruple.' As with the great works of avant-garde art, the fascination of this politics of hardness, a politics 'without pain, without guilty conscience,' lies in the shocking features of amorality. Such a politics, conceived from the perspective of its own limiting case, has of course a singular advantage over art in that it lends a certain existential quality to aesthetic experience. It shelters the last reserve of the extraordinary in the flatland of banalized everyday life, and merges with the aura of the strong state. In the end, then, 'forty years of political abstinence' explains the 'Federal Republic's horror of reconciliation,' which can bear no more hardness.[14]

These are all elements that bob to the surface from the 'anticivilizational, anti-Western undercurrent of the German tradition' (Adorno). Cobbling these elements together into arguments against a new German special consciousness is really a kind of con artistry. Our author asks the peace movement 'whether the grandchildren of the Nazis would stand on the side of the enemies of democracy for a second time.' Such a question ought to be off limits for the sons of Ernst Jünger, Carl Schmitt, and Martin Heidegger, men who sought to lure us back into the extraordinary rites of the 'boldness of *Dasein*' with the bloated longing for hardness and weight. No normalcy – certainly not that of the Anglo-Saxon democracies – is going to be foisted on us through this aestheticization of the political.

The Normative Deficits of Unification

MICHAEL HALLER: *We're speaking about the special histor-ical situation of Germany since the late fall of 1989. Let's turn now to the second great event, the unification of the two Ger-manies, an event that for us Germans has produced both eu-phoria and also new anxieties.*

Within the space of twelve months, our political landscape has changed more radically than over the preceding forty years. The image of the East German state vanished as sud-denly as if it were a kind of fata morgana. Is the disappearance of the GDR nothing more than the downfall of an unjust regime, or have the Germans 'over there' in the East also lost some-thing that for them – or perhaps even for us as well – would have been worth keeping?

»«

JÜRGEN HABERMAS: The overthrow of an unjust regime, the liberation from globally penetrating surveillance by a secret police that shadowed everyone with a dogged and cold-blooded perfection – the panoptical society that Fou-cault had already discerned in our own social reality – is in normative terms the decisive element of the revolution. To-day we have the octopus as the symbol for this kind of domination organized with the best German thoroughness and professionalism, an image expressing the feeling of all those affected that the demise of the GDR isn't a matter of one single act of liberation, but rather a detoxification pro-cess of unknown duration. A dragon has been slain; the octopus is dead – but it doesn't let go of everything in its grip. Therefore some things survive that really aren't worth preserving. This new beginning is saddled with false continuities – just as the beginning of the Federal Republic was in its day. As with us, a portion of questionable mentality seems to have been preserved along with the 'old boys' network' – back then we didn't even have a plastic word for it.[1] But you're asking about what's *worth* preserving.

What's worth preserving isn't to be found at the institutional level. The economy was unproductive. The administrative institutions were an apparatus of repression. There was an advanced degree of delegitimation, at least among the younger generations. Even the social system's core of legitimation, a low-level social security bought with concealed unemployment, was rotten: it was housed inside a shell that, as Marx would say, kept all the forces of production in fetters. But you'd have to ask someone else – Konrad Weiss, Friedrich Schorlemmer, Bischof Forck, Bärbel Boley, et al. – about what kinds of experiences, mentalities, or lifestyles *below* the institutional level might be worth salvaging from the forty-year history of the GDR.[2]

I come from a small protestant corner of Rhein-Preußen, very far from Berlin. My family had no relatives over in the East. As a student in the early 1950s, I went a few times to the Schiffbauer-Damm Theater as long as Brecht wasn't allowed to be performed where we were. A little later on, in 1954–55, we also had some contact with an FDJ agency in East Berlin that loaned us DEFA films for our student film club in Bonn.[3] On the same occasion I also went to Humboldt University to visit the old seminar of my teacher Nicolai Hartmann. Those were the few contacts I had with the 'official' world over in the East, which seemed as strange, as horrifying, and as authoritarian to me as the guards at the

34

Friedrichstrasse subway station.[4] I didn't come into contact with this world again for another thirty-five years. I received a first invitation in 1988 from a colleague in Halle. In the summer of 1988 I delivered a lecture under the watchful eye of the chief philosopher of the GDR, who had traveled from Berlin just for this purpose – a truly absurd 'supervision' when you consider the point in time. I had just as little contact with oppositional groups. I mention these stories of a kind of relationlessness in order to recall that we in the West have more in common with the postwar histories of Italy, or France, or the United States, than we do with that of the GDR. For my children and their generation, this is particularly true. It's in the light of this fact that we have to understand the remarks (condemned as unjust) of the chief of cultural affairs in Frankfurt, in whose life, trivially, Milan must have had a far greater meaning than Leipzig. It's something you have to grasp without sentimentalism.

On the other hand, I lived my first fifteen years in the German – indeed the 'Greater German' – *Reich*. That is why the events since 9 November 1989 are still able to awaken personal memories—of summer vacations in Warnemünde, Zinnowitz, or Rügen, for example. How much stronger and richer such memories must be for others, who maintained connections 'over there' beyond the end of the war. Everybody perceived the opening of the Wall – and in hindsight the unification of the two German states as well – as the end of an artificial separation. For older people, it was also true that such perceptions were nourished by the unpolitical memories of the normality of everyday life during the Nazi years. For all those who still possessed such personal memories, the nearly forgotten artificiality of the conditions – and above all the mode – of Germany's division came as a true shock. For all the others, younger than fifty, the map of the 'new states' is a blank slate.

Naturally, for a German philosopher who came to maturity in that tradition, Jena has the kind of aura that perhaps Oxford or Cambridge has for my English colleagues, or Harvard for the Americans. But intellectual traditions detach themselves from their geographical origins. The circumstance that Königsberg is now known as Kaliningrad doesn't alter the meaning that Kant has for us. If one opens a tourism book about Saxony today, it's the cityscapes, the castles, the ruined landscapes and markets, and the fallen-in baroque houses that one is curious about. That the book also reclaims Leibniz, Lessing, or Wagner as 'Saxons of Greatness,' like something out of an advertising supplement, doesn't add much – except maybe for a mild surprise – to what we already knew about the European Lessing and Leibniz or (God help us) Bayreuth. The ownership of cultural traditions persists in other ways than through the political possession of territory. It would have been nice to be able just to visit the 150 square meters of immortal German cultural history at the old cemetery at Jena, but for *that,* all that would have been required was normal tourist traffic between normal neighbors. We've witnessed a kind of land-grabbing territorial fetishism over the last year, as if we could appropriate some ground of tradition by restructuring the GDR. These triumphal tones sounded over a supposedly spiritual greatness have made me rather nervous.

So I can't say much in response to your question about what is worth keeping and worth remembering in the former GDR. For many of its citizens the downfall of the GDR is bringing losses with it as well – and not only in jobs and lifestyles. Modernization processes always brutally devalue the past. Most importantly, however, the demise of the GDR stirs up *other* pasts, whether we have personal memories of the prehistory or not, including pasts that ought not to serve as models for the future, pasts that shouldn't regain any power over the present.

»«

Despite economic bankruptcy, the Stasi, and the political rhetoric of the SED,[5] *the former* GDR *always wanted, at least, to be a more progressive country than West Germany in the fields of pacifist politics and social issues. Was this self-deception? Propaganda? Or were these worthwhile national political goals?*

»«

The political rhetoric of the 'workers' and farmers' state' was a misuse of progressive ideas in the service of political self-legitimation, cynically denying these ideals through its inhuman praxis and thus bringing them into disrepute. I'm afraid that this dialectic of devaluation will end up being more ruinous for the spiritual hygiene of Germany than all the concentrated resentment of five or six generations of antienlightenment, anti-Semitic, false romantic, jingoistic obscurantists. The devaluation of our best and most fragile intellectual traditions is, for me, one of the most evil aspects of the legacy that the GDR brings into the expanded Federal Republic. It's a destruction of reason that Lukács never dreamed of.[6] It's clear that reified, textbook dialectical materialism [*Lehrbuch-DiaMat*] was from the beginning a legitimating ideology tailored to Stalin's Soviet imperialism. But until 1953 the emigrants who had returned to the GDR from the West, such as Brecht, Bloch, Hans Mayer, Stefan Heym, or others such as Anna Seghers, testified to the GDR's willingness, at least on the surface, to stand up for those progressive traditions that had always had a particularly rough time in Germany. This pretension of representing the better Germany had blank spaces: no Freud, no Kafka, no Wittgenstein, no Nietzsche. But the East German publishing houses' claim to represent the tradition of Heine – a kind of resolute enlightenment – was all the more emphatic inasmuch as the antifascism that had characterized the first years of West Germany – think of Kogon's *SS State,* of Langhoff's *Moorsoldaten* or Weisenborn's *Memorial,* which were being performed in Frankfurt, Munich, or Hamburg – had to yield almost immediately to the same old obligatory anticommunism that supplied the motifs for Adenauer's election posters.

If you're asking me about the normative orientations that are worth preserving, you have to think back not so much to the GDR of the Free German Youth and party convention speeches as to the GDR of the early DEFA films, to some of the publishing programs from the early 1950s, or to a span of one or two generations of left-wing oppositional writers extending to Heiner Müller and Christoph Hein. But at the same time one has to see that this high counterculture was mutilated from the very beginning by the censorship of a truly despicable cultural politics, and that a mandatory realism made any appropriation of the subversive spirit of radical modernism difficult if not impossible. Nevertheless, the one was so intertwined with the other that today it requires a tremendous differentiating effort to keep the traditions that in both Germanies have been renewed and borne by the spirit of antifascism from falling into acrimony. Now there's no shortage of cultural luminaries ready to take the downfall of the GDR as a pretext for hustling to gloss over everything that doesn't fit into the elitist model of a specifically German cultural pessimism deeply rooted in historicist, late romantic thought. I'm afraid something of that old sour atmosphere is going to be seeping back in, and the 'cultured' will replace the 'intellectuals' once again. We've already spoken of the young conservative contempt for the *juste milieu*.

» «

Thinking back to that week in November 1989 when the Wall came down and the people of East and West fell into each other's arms, please tell us how you experienced what's since been named the 'turn' [Wende]? What observations did you make of this transformation?

» «

You too use the expression 'turn,' an expression that was first coined by Genscher as a way of toppling the Schmidt administration and bringing Helmut Kohl to power. It's a dead giveaway that the population of the former GDR talks about a 'turn' when they describe the fall of the SED regime. Our fellow citizens in the East don't seem to have the feeling that they made a revolution – or even that they were present at one. The revolution interpretation was something we Westerners pressed on them – perhaps to cover the need for remedial work, for making up for lost time, a need that Marx had already noted. More respectable voices proudly hearken back to Hegel, who held that the Reformation had made political revolutions superfluous for Protestant countries. Whatever the case may be, the historians will instruct us whether it was indeed a remedial revolution, or simply a transformation, a transition, a systemic change brought about by the phased process of self-destruction of a superpower. The more specifics we learn about the inner constitution of the GDR before November and the course of events leading up to the (obviously unplanned) opening of the Wall, the more clearly the accidental character of events and the passivity of the social movements emerge. Today one wouldn't even be completely shocked anymore if Markus Wolf announced that Honecker had fallen victim to a conspiracy of the State Security.[7] The locus of control doesn't seem to have been located within the engaged, demonstrating masses and their brave and civil leaders nearly to the extent that it appeared, at first, from the exciting images of the omnipresent television cameras.

On the whole, more happening than initiative – over the course of the past year, this impression has grown steadily stronger. A lot has contributed to it: a certain degree of helplessness and confusion on the part of the initiators, who were quickly pushed out of the way; a lack of self-consciousness and self-respect, a kind of cheap selling of the self of many people in the GDR; a more sharply critical assessment of the nonconformity, resistance, and opposition of a population that, no matter how unwillingly, had managed to accommodate itself to the practices of a not-so-secret Secret Police; and finally, that awful fusion of culprit and victim in one and the same person, for which de Mazière has become the symbol.[8] Whether he's being treated justly now or not, symbols have a historical effect: the first freely elected minister president, who gave an unforgettable inauguration speech in the *Volkskammer,* was, as the suspected 'Czerny,' forced to give up his post in the federal government. In retrospect, these depressing aspects have robbed a transformation that anyone would have greeted with enthusiasm of much of its aura. Images of liberation and of capitulation telescope into one another; what's left behind is the mournful fact that, of all the data that have brashly been declared as 'historical,' hardly one of them will impress itself on the collective memory of coming generations. What happened at the beginning was purity of feeling, a moment of solidarity and joy, indeed a glimpse of the sublime for everyone who empathized with the elated celebration on the television screen; the utterly civil enthusiasm of the streams of East Germans rushing westward, reclaiming their immediate physical freedom. I'm afraid that no historically lasting memories will crystallize from this emotional beginning. The events may well have objectively brought about a 'turn,' but weren't able to complete it from out of that consciousness that first appeared on the scene with the French Revolution.

I suspect that the mode of the unification process itself is more important: historical events are interpreted retrospectively. The mode and the tempo of the unification process have been dictated by the federal government. The most striking physiognomic feature of this is the instrumental character of the administrative procedure itself. Despite all the carefully installed foreign-policy cushioning, despite all the tailoring to economic imperatives, this procedure never won any *democratic* dynamic of its own. The journalists praised the government for seizing the 'hour of the executive.' But the truth is that Kohl and his kitchen cabinet achieved their goals with the same kind of virtues and vices that one would have only expected from the narrow political infighting over some issue of domestic policy. By the instrumental use of international treaties, policies of self-imposed deadlines, and the commandeering of the organizational networks of the bloc parties,[9] they managed to out-maneuver both the deeply divided opposition and the public sphere. They set the course for a process that proceeded primarily in the categories of economic organization – without ever having made the political alternatives into a theme for discussion. Of course, circumstances cooperated, and by this I don't just mean a foreign-policy situation that was as urgent as it was lucky. The single decision of political substance concerned the timing and the modality of the currency reform, and that one was made so early – and despite the misgivings of the economic elites and the advice of the *Bundesbank* – because voter attitudes in the approaching election campaign for the *Volkskammer* made conditions highly favorable for the CDU.[10] Lambsdorff, Kohl, and their fixers conceived of the unification process as the task of the legal and administrative reorganization of a self-running economic mechanism. Naturally, a very naïve kind of economic liberalism was also responsible for the grotesque miscalculation that the unchecked play of market forces would be able to bring off this reorganization, which could only have been achieved through a reconstructive process handled with political kid gloves. But one shouldn't so naïvely underestimate what one could call the Dreggerian consciousness of being able to make 'great' politics at the great moment of national history.[11] A good bit of the nineteenth century was at work in the heads of these movers and shakers, who indeed otherwise are remarkable for their unremarkableness.

All this corresponds to the logic of a situation that Claus Offe[12] has analyzed well. Despite all the ideological measures it took for its national independence, the GDR was only able to develop an economic national identity. It represented something like the pure, archetypical form of a bureaucratic-socialistic economic society. Thus, in contrast to a country such as Hungary, the systemic changes in the

GDR could not be completed from within the framework of a nation-state grounded in the continuity of its own historical experiences. In Offe's words, 'The transformation in the GDR is a matter of the revolution that was made possible, and delimited, by entering the constitutional system of the Federal Republic. But constitutional change was not the driving force or the guiding motive of the coup.' Among the supports for this thesis is the observation that, unlike Poland or Czechoslovakia, the GDR possessed no visible counterelites and counterorganizations standing by to replace the old regime with their own reformist perspectives. 'The revolution in the GDR was an exit revolution, not a voice revolution. The end of the state of the GDR was brought about not by a victorious collective struggle for a new political order but by the destruction of its economic base through the massive and suddenly uncontrollable emigration of individuals.' This stark formulation surely doesn't do justice to the intentions of the citizens' movements and the courageous demonstrators of the first hours. And yet the Round Table, the sole institutional embodiment of political resistance in the GDR, was not only a stone in the path of the politics of destabilization and annexation of the (West German) federal government; even in the GDR itself the Round Table never won any authority.[13] In a real appraisal of the motives that moved the people, the newly elected *Volkskammer* never even discussed the draft constitution, the only place that the pathos and the normative perspectives of a new beginning had taken shape.

On the other side, the population of the Federal Republic also looked on the unification process astonishingly soberly – that is, from a predominantly economic point of view. Lafontaine didn't come up with the theme of the 'costs of unity' from thin air.[14] As a way of responding to the 'cost-conscious reserve' of West German burghers, the federal government held out the dangerous promise that all the additional costs of unification could be financed by taking on debt, rather than through new taxes. At the time, this unwillingness to present the West German public with tough choices was roundly criticized as timid and partisan. But it proves that the government was dealing with a population that perceived the unification process in the same terms as it did itself – as a shrewdly prepared administrative act creating the legal provisions for the implementation of market mechanisms along with their corresponding social 'cushions.'[15] Unification hasn't been understood as a normatively willed act of the citizens of both states, who in political self-awareness decided on a common civil union. This is shown by the arguments that the 'Wessis' used to convince the 'Ossis' of the modality and all-too-crudely seized opportunity for an admission into the Federal Republic according to Article 23 of the Basic Law, and by the near-hysterical fear of a forum on the constitution itself, a discussion that is even constitutionally mandated according to Article 146.[16] With a very few notable exceptions, including the constitutional jurists Grimm and Simon, the rest of the German federal lawyers – buoyed by the press, itself a major support of the government – proved themselves once again to be the zealous underlings for the legitimation of those in power.

» «

The heavy criticisms that have been directed at the 'forced march' unification policies of the Kohl administration raise the question of whether there really were any practical alternatives to the 'heave-ho unification' of 1990. Were there such al-

ternatives? Or was it simply the case, as the liberal publicists write, that in the end unification was the result of a purely practical reason that set its sights on what was realistically possible, and that then went ahead contrary to all utopian expectations?

» «

Until now the story that there were no alternatives to the course and the tempo of the unification process has been carefully tended. Parliamentary elections don't answer questions of this kind. In my view, the three most important arguments offered in support of this story are false, or at least debatable. First is the argument concerning the numbers of East Germans emigrating into the West: these numbers were certainly real, but they were also manipulated. A realistic estimate of the high end of the figures on new emigrants would have made it much less frightening and dramatic. At present I suspect that just as many qualified workers are emigrating to the West as before the currency union. They're now talking about twenty thousand new emigrants per month. As far as the second, economic argument is concerned – the argument that the collapse of the economic system in the GDR had become unstoppable – a reference to the status quo is enough. The destruction of productive capacities and jobs that we *now* have could well have been avoided, at least on this scale, by a 'slow path' in which the government controlled the pace of the transition process with subsidized rest periods. The chief problem of an unforced unification process would have been the maintenance of tariff and customs borders. But in view of the reluctance to make capital investments in the new states, the dilemma the federal government now faces was clear from the very beginning. Using the medium of constitutional law to heave our countrymen into our own boat by the scruff of their necks meant that the constitutional norm of comparable standards of living had to open up a gap between the cost of wages and productivity levels – a gap that according to the laws of a market economy has a counterproductive effect. Third and most convincing is the argument from a foreign-policy perspective, according to which the 'favorable hour' for unification arrived and had to be seized. But this argument too has lost much of its force in the meantime. The Warsaw Pact would have fallen apart one way or another. And the Supreme Soviet gave its approval to the so-called 2 + 4 treaty[17] even though Gorbachev was already in deep trouble.

In another sense, these sorts of counterfactual backward glances into history and politics are always awkward. Today these discussions don't make very much sense. It's no use crying over spilled milk. But I don't find it appropriate in this context to counterpose 'practical reason' and 'utopia' – there is a normative as well as a pragmatic use of practical reason.

» «

And it's obviously this normative use that is relevant for you. From this perspective, then: of the objections to the unification process that you and other intellectuals expressed at the time, which do you regard as still relevant now in 1991?

» «

The intellectuals have complained about the normative deficit of the unification process. I regard this as important, because it's a complaint about the reckless intervention in our political culture, and thus about long-term damages to it that the political parties dangerously ignored in their election tactics, and the bureaucrats ignored with the administrative institutionalization of an economic system. The institutions provided for by the Basic Law can only function as well as they are allowed by the civil consciousness of a population *accustomed* to institutions of freedom. Political culture is made up of a delicate fabric of mentalities and convictions that can neither be invented nor manipulated through administrative measures. What we're objecting to is the reckless treatment of incalculable and exhaustible moral and cultural resources – resources that can regenerate themselves only spontaneously, and not according to a prearranged path. Self-understanding, the political self-consciousness of a nation of citizens, forms itself only in the medium of public communication. And this communication depends on a cultural infrastructure that is at this moment being allowed to fall into ruins in the new states.

In fact, the administrative 'liquidation' of universities, colleges, and museums, and the conversion of theater, film, and literature to the Westernized models of market and subsidy, are in effect even worse than the destruction of productive capacities in other sectors. Intellectual capacities can no longer be regenerated when the production is interrupted for two, three, or five generations. Foreshortened biographies are *always* a catastrophe. But industrial capacities can be replaced by other means. Decayed cultural milieus can't be rebuilt in the same way. Once they're ruined, they're ruined for good.

» «

In the Frankfurter Allgemeine Zeitung *your colleagues have accused you of trying to invent a new 'stab in the back' legend with your criticisms of the German unification process (FAZ, 19 December 1990).*[18]

That's a grotesque and willfully malicious reversal. After World War I the myth of 'betrayal on the homefront' contributed to the destabilization of the Weimar Republic. The criticisms that I and many others have expressed are directed precisely against the undervaluing and the impoverishment of the political and cultural reserves that a democratic legal state must stay rooted in, if it is to remain stable. But let me address the tone of doubt in some of your questions.

In hindsight, for example, I recognize that as a student, and in the years immediately thereafter, I didn't have an adequate assessment of the historical consequences of Adenauer's great achievement – binding the Federal Republic strongly with the Western alliance and the Western social system. When I was eligible to vote for the first time, in the *Bundestag* elections of 1953, I cast my second ballot for the GVP, Heinemann's party. With the first ballot I gritted my teeth and voted for the Schumacher SPD, which was far too national for my taste.[19] Adenauer – the politics of normalization of an old man with a limited vocabulary – made my hair stand on end. Not only was he completely out of touch with the experiences and expectations of the younger generations, but he was also utterly insensitive to the kind of mental damage that was the cost of a restoration of attitudes – and not just attitudes – that throve under his wing. Maybe the political and moral costs of the coldly calculated reintegration of the old Pg's, and of his own hurry to fall in line on the remilitarization question, were just things he put up with as a part of the bargain.[20] Nevertheless, our radical opposition to this spirit of the Adenauer era appears to me to be still justified. Without the opposition of the left-liberals – and occasionally even of the left intelligentsia (which formed itself at this time and developed a certain infectious force only later, during the incubation period of the student movements of the early 1960s) – without this division of labor between those in power and their 'tweakers,' a sense of *zivilizierter Bürgersinn,* or a civic mentality as such, would never have been able to develop in the Federal Republic. My feeling is that this new mentality was embodied in the state apparatus for the first time in the figure of *Bundespräsident* Heinemann. Without this 'double rule' between restorational politics and the oppositional intelligentsia, things would have been left to the sheer 'trust in the system' of a successful economy. Neoconservative vaporings plus phony baroque would never have conspired to produce a deep identification with a social order whose universalistic principles anchor a potential for self-criticism and self-transformation.

But let's assume, for a moment, that I'm fooling myself again over the historical meaning of what appears to me to be Kohl's politics of annexation. Let's assume further that, as your questions imply, there were no alternatives to this politics. Let's assume for the sake of argument that Kohl even had some awareness of the political and cultural uncertainties and the moral costs of this politics, and that he simply accepted them as an unavoidable part of the deal – even assuming all this, it would still be a case of *dereliction* for the intellectuals not to call attention to the enormous damage that's been done. It's not the political union itself but the mode of this union that's being criticized. Let me draw your attention to three things.

First of all, there was the new dimension of the way that a political past was brought to consciousness, a past in which an *entire* population is horribly entangled thanks to the domination of the Stasis. In fact, many of the arguments in favor of a slower tempo for the unification process were not just trying to give the citizens of the GDR some time for self-reflection and for confronting their own past; the arguments were asking for the construction of the very conditions that would permit an autonomous encounter with these kinds of delicate problems. If such problems aren't faced in one's own house, from one's own initiative, and under one's own power, they become unsolvable. Public debates over collective self-understanding – which always contain a high potential for injuries on both sides – gain legitimacy only on the basis of a common, shared history, under the presupposition that the one side knows what the other side is talking about because it has had the same ambivalent experiences, because it possesses the same intimate, still barely articulated knowledge. Richard Schröder, the theologian and former SPD leader in the *Volkskammer*, asks us whether the Stasi's work of social corrosion and disunity is going to go on forever, with the help of the Western media: 'The problem has to be publicly discussed. But by whom? . . . It's precisely here in the Stasi problem that Westerners lack something unrecoverable: they didn't experience it all themselves. . . . They have to let us tell them how it was, and at least listen, even if it's hard. And after this turbulent year, we Easterners have to make the effort to remember correctly how we lived and thought before this year, before the revelations broke over us' (*FAZ*, 2 January 1991).

Schröder's plea is reminiscent of the denazification process in what was then the Western Zone, and why this process (among others) went askew: the civil population felt itself misunderstood by the Occupation Forces and thus dealt with whatever was imposed on them purely strate-gically. But there are no Occupation Forces for the new states. Instead they face the accusing fingers of their own fellow countrymen, who had been saved from the same fate only through luck and circumstance. How could a pop-ulation humiliated two times over (after 1933 and since 1949) hope to cultivate a political self-consciousness, when something they have to do for themselves is taken over by agents from the outside? In a late act of self-defense against this *third* humiliation, the *Volkskammer* was able, literally at the last hour, to keep the Stasi files from falling into the hands of the West Germans. In the meantime the East Ger-man special envoy to the federal government, the civil ju-rist Joachim Gauck, was obliged to fight against the CDU's unreasonable demand to load his own staff with experts on the protection of the West German constitution. The strug-gle over the 'File Law' does not bode well for the future.[21] The same problem turns up again in relation to the juridic 'liquidation' of entire institutions. One need not even go into the embarrassing details, for example the moral ob-scenity of the task now occupying countless Western com-missions, as they submit their Eastern colleagues in col-leges, universities, courts, administrations, and service sec-tors to job evaluations combined with political attitude tests.

The poisoned atmosphere generated by this transfer of the moral 'rubbish heap' into West German management doesn't just concern the one side. For us managers, now cast in the role of judge in this waste-disposal project, it's all too easy to take the widely practiced game of clean break–making [*Schlußstriche-Ziehens*] to a whole new level. To-day we don't calculate Stalin's crimes against Hitler's any-more. As experts in management of the past, we need only

issue a report on somebody else's catastrophes. *That* was
what Günter Grass was afraid of when he brought Auschwitz into the discussion. You can't respond to him with the
valid but irrelevant argument that the division of Germany
wasn't the political consequence of the death camps.[22]

Secondly, a lot of criticism has been directed at the democratic or civil deficiency of the unification process that I've
already mentioned. The constitutional discussion was regarded as an obstacle to the smooth operation of the administration and pushed to the side. Those who demanded it
were laughed at as utopians, or were saddled, as usual, with
the reputation of a lack of loyalty to the constitution. But is
it actually so unrealistic to think to what in the middle term
will pay off in the currency of civic sense and political culture – or otherwise in social polarizations? The Basic Law
had made provisions for an institutionalized process for
the creation of a constitution for the given case. Was it so
utopian to expect that the federal government, or at least
the SPD, would take up the impulses set in motion by the
Round Table – impulses that now are continued only by a
board of trustees for a democratically constituted federation of German states? Is it too much to demand that an
effort be made in the medium of public communication, so
that a *new* Federal Republic, composed of such unequal
parts, can anchor itself in the consciousness of its citizens
as something shared – and not experienced just as the by-
product of the forced construction of an expanded currency zone?

Naturally, state unification has been legitimized through
democratic elections. But the mode of East Germany's entrance into the Federal Republic deprived four-fifths of eligible voters of the chance to make a free choice. They simply haven't been asked: they could only confirm the annex-

ation as a fait accompli, in a downcast *Bundestag* election with correspondingly low voter turnout. The normative deficit consists in the fact that, apart from stupid election slogans like 'We rejoice in Germany,' the 'political class' made no effort to win over the majority of West German voters (who are too young to have much connection with the rather alien GDR) for the difficult project of creating a common nation of citizens. A similar deficit has arisen on the other side, because apart from a hasty whitewashing for the 'Alliance for Germany,'[23] nobody ever bothered to make the normative content of the principles of democracy and state legality embodied in the Basic Law accessible to the mass of the population of the GDR who have no memory of the years before 1933. That, in any case, was the critical meaning of Schily's banana.[24]

Instead, the politicians settled on national feeling – a third point. Naturally, Kohl and Waigel[25] also knew that demands for prosperity alone couldn't bring about the integration of the political system. Claus Offe has referred to the peculiarly artificial character of this new nationalism; he speaks of a coldly calculated 'elite nationalism,' shoved into place as a meaning-giving support column for the rushed process of economic integration. In the West, at least, one could actually observe the nationalist tones issuing far more from the mouths of politicians than from the beer halls. When one considers that nationalism always has something manipulative attached to it, the generally moderate tone of these calls is reassuring. I regard it as a bit of luck within misfortune that the conservative majority had made up its mind long before the *Bundestag* election; as a consequence, the right-wing parties were never tempted to drop their foreign-policy considerations and grab deeper into the vocabulary of nationalism.

A discussion determined by ethical and political viewpoints would have been appropriate here, instead of fooling the voters into thinking that unification could be financed without raising taxes. There ought to have been an appeal to those who drew a better lot through the accident of their birthplace, an appeal for solidarity with the others who were imprisoned by the Soviet victors for the barbarities committed in the war. An understanding could have been awakened for the resulting problem for our Eastern European neighbors: that the frontier of prosperity is now simply to be moved to the Oder-Neisse line. There could have been a test of the delicate balance that has to be maintained between our special responsibilities toward our fellow countrymen versus our solidarity with Eastern Europe, only now liberating itself under hard economic conditions. But this issue was at best touched on only by our *Bundespräsident*. The others handled the program according to the transparent logic of the election campaigns and dressed up the signs of enlightened self-interest in the clichés of fake nationalist affectations. They relied on the national stereotypes, but not the normative dispositions, of West German citizens. There are certainly arguments in favor of a cleverly instrumental praxis. It's only the disparity between this praxis and the grand, empty words that makes the embracing-exploiting style of the new German way of doing business so unappetizing.

I don't recall these directions of criticism to belabor the point. The unification process has now run its course in conformity with the scenario of the chancellor's office. But I'm incorrigible enough to believe that the problems that are approaching us can be managed better if we take account of the normative deficit of this far too hasty journey.

The Past as Future

MICHAEL HALLER: *Let's now turn from the political system to society. The new perspectives and new expectations born in the winter of 1989–90, especially in the East, changed over to bitter disappointment once the unification process was complete. Let's recall that in November 1989 the masses took to the streets for a rejuvenated socialism; only a few months later there was practically no more talk of it. What kinds of new opinions, ideas, and interests have emerged in the wake of what Helmut Kohl has labeled his* Deutschlandpolitik? *And who, in the end, will profit from it?*

» «

JÜRGEN HABERMAS: What new opinions, interests, and ideas emerge from Kohl's *Deutschlandpolitik*? The structural collapse of the former GDR will result in clear winners and losers. The price of admission into a market economy has to be paid in the currency of social inequity, entirely new kinds of social divisions, and in higher long-term unemployment. A relatively higher level of base unemployment will persist in the new states, because one segment of the population is too old, and another too poorly trained, for a cognitively adequate and spiritually robust reaction to the considerable pressure for adaptation. As is always the case in accelerated social transformation, crises get shifted onto the life histories, onto the psychic and physical health of individuals. The high suicide rate in the new states is a signal of this. Moreover, those who were favored with relatively unegregious advantages of position under the old system will still have an advantage over others under the new conditions due to their organizational head start and their competence – as one can see in the second and third levels of the old bloc parties. Even Stasi collaborators are occasionally privileged, insofar as they have access to potentially destabilizing kinds of information. For the remainder, the new apportioning of privileges is not being played out according to any calculable pattern. The connections that prove to be advantageous are often accidental.

Now that the course of the unification process has been set, it's pretty obvious who's going to profit from it in the West. I don't mean the petty crooks who pocketed the 'windfall profits,' so much as the large corporations that expanded their capacities during the first phases of the transition and then went on to take over East German markets without investing there and creating jobs on site. For the West German economy, the currency reform has functioned so far as a giant, credit-financed federal program of economic speculation. In general, and for the medium term, it can be said that the economic policies embodied by Lambsdorff will be able to be carried out rather more recklessly than in the past.[1] The 4.5 percent rate of annual economic growth that was forecast for 1991 also means a growth of social inequity, namely, mounting profits from falling wages. It means an even more sharply segmented society: while the rich get richer, the poor not only get poorer, but more and more of the poor will be pushed out of the system and into the underclasses, where they will have no access to veto power and won't be able to improve their situation through their own efforts. In a word: the social climate is going to get a lot colder.

Even taking into account the setbacks they suffered as a

result of the extreme disappointment over the never-materialized economic boom in the new states, the conservative parties are also profiting from the transformation of public opinion. The reconstruction of the economy of the GDR – and in general the whole range of problems that arose along with the liquidation, reorganization, and construction of important functional sectors, as well as the control of social tensions and anomic potentials in the new states – pushed into the background a number of issues that, in the prosperous Federal Republic, had become increasingly prominent in public consciousness prior to the unification process. I'm referring to the issues that the New Social Movements had presented under the sign of 'postmaterial' value orientations. In fact, the old Federal Republic was well on the way toward a modern democratic society with strengthened political participation, and toward a protest culture that reminded the 'two-thirds society'[2] of the new tasks of the social and ecological domestication of capitalism (that is, of an economic system sensitive to its own external costs), and of new strategies beyond the privileged administrative forms of state-social pacification. The tertiarization of the economy, favorable economic trends, the expansion of the educational system, and the by and large progressive transformation of motives and attitudes had created conditions favorable for all this.

And yet, well past November 1989, the Lafontaine-led SPD, which had taken on these new tasks in the form of the Berlin Plan,[3] was still able to entertain reasonable hopes of replacing the federal government with a Red-Green coalition.[4] The elections of the past year have signaled a reversal of trends. But the trends aren't just snapped because other problems were pushed objectively into the foreground. Researchers of value changes empirically confirm the impression one had anyway: there is a mentality predominating in the new states that we recognize from the Adenauer period. The GDR has not yet caught up with the dramatic transformation of value orientations that has taken place in the Federal Republic since the late 1960s. So it's not surprising that voter preference in the unified Germany is divided up differently.

The last parliamentary elections overturned the emergent majorities of the old Federal Republic and provided the conservative forces with a drastic and perhaps long-term overbalance. As residents of an economically, socio-politically, and ecologically backward country, the East Germans were confronted with the televised fair-weather model of the political and social system of the Federal Republic. They voted for the fatuous promise that standards of living in both parts of the new Germany would be quickly brought in line with one another. The pull toward conservatism is intensified through the authoritarian potential that, according to all comprehensive survey data, is more deeply embedded in the former GDR than in the Federal Republic (so far). These differences in mentality between East and West have resulted in a change in the composition of the voter basis of both of the large parties – in the East, the majority of the working class voted for the CDU. The gains of the FDP in both parts show that attitudes toward economic liberalism were still good in December. But even despite the missing economic upturn, the reconstructionist mentality of the 1950s will receive a boost. These are very rough indicators for a sea change that, of course, appears less univocal when one takes the widening generation gap into account. Younger people have other interests and feelings, other life orientations than the cartel of politicians in Bonn who are setting the tone – now that the Greens are gone from the parliament, and after the innovators in the SPD, who seriously intend the ecological reconfiguration of industrial society, have had to scale back their plans.

» «

So much for the interests and currents in the wider population. The intellectual landscape has also been peculiarly transformed. Are the intellectuals really as helpless in the arena of national politics as they are accused of being, particularly by conservatives?

» «

New debates were being opened up long before the Gulf War – as early as November 1989. At that time, an influential article appeared under the title 'The Silence of the Clerks': a reference to the old story that the intellectuals, particularly on the left, lapsed into a 'threatening silence' – as one reads it a year later in the *Suddeutsche Zeitung*.[5] A quick glance through the pile of newspaper clippings that has collected on my desk over the past year teaches the opposite. Indeed, it would be virtually incomprehensible if a process of this magnitude didn't release a flood of public discussions. The only thing meager about it was the mummified words of the actors themselves. The only bit of boilerplate that our cliché-ridden chancellor could come up with was the tautology that the events were 'historic.' We might as well let this pass. But in the parliament as well, there was barely a complete sentence to be found. The single speech of any rhetorical value and political substance was given by Antje Vollmer.[6] Against this gray background, the intellectuals don't end up looking all that bad. Hardly any of them remained silent. The legend of the – embarrassed? – silence of the intellectuals is hiding something like a discontent that the leftists among them failed to register the proper enthusiasm.

Of course I'm astonished that Ralf Dahrendorf [7] joined in to this chorus. He regards it as more than just a minor problem that the country's intellectuals don't go along with the whole trend. 'If the politicians are lacking the words, then at least the speaking and writing guilds ought to find them. Instead, the guilds sow doubt' (*Merkur,* October/November 1990, 825). This talk of the 'failure of the intellectuals' is all the more astonishing coming from Dahrendorf, since he himself pointed out the 'constitutional status of the event' and thus to the normative and legal dimension, which nevertheless in the view of the scolded intellectuals was utterly ignored by the short-sighted management strategies of the authorities. Moreover, Dahrendorf operates with the same distinction between the nation as prepolitical magnitude and the institutionally constituted nation of citizens under equal rights, grounded through an act of will, that I had insisted on six months earlier: 'German unity is a constitutional task; a task of the creation of civil rights and the conditions of a civil society. Only in this way can "citizenship" and "civil society" regain an unambiguously radical and liberal significance that, in their German versions, they last had in the *Vormärz* period.'[8] *This* is what was really at issue, particularly if one takes seriously the objection that Dahrendorf himself raises: 'If the developments of the last year imply a turn in which homogenous nations take the place of civil societies and old national rivalries take over from what was sketched out as a European and ultimately a world civil society, then the time has come for liberals to justify their positions loudly and clearly.'

The left had still more reasons for its skepticism: concepts like 'civil society' and 'citizenship' raise other kinds of associations for it than for the old liberals of the *Vormärz*. These ideas, rediscovered (not coincidentally) by dissidents, acted as a stimulant for the West European left, for whom 'civil society' means something like the societal basis for a vital form of public communication operating between state and economy as a medium that preserves citizenship itself. And yet the relation of the West European left to dissidents in the East is not without tension and ironies, as Andrew Arato[9] has noted: 'For the liberals among the ranks of the former democratic opposition in Eastern Europe, the European past itself serves as a model; for the Social Democrats, the model is the European present. But what about all those who critically opposed both this past and this present, both economic liberalism and the social state? What kinds of useful perspectives can they offer, now that all the future-oriented experiments have proven themselves to be merely surfeit? If this is truly the case, then the only thing to be learned from it is to value what we already have, or to wish for what already lies behind us, or at best to strive for what the Swedes have – exercises that, for some of us, are no more attractive now than they ever were' (*Transit* 1[1990]: 111). Arato describes our situation thoroughly self-critically: the left ought to find new responses to a new situation, instead of buying in to liberal complacency.

» «

Those are unusual demands, considering that the traditional left always saw its mission as offering criticism, rather than positive solutions. What sort of new answers do you think our left is capable of?

» «

At least the left knows *that* it has to learn – even if it doesn't exactly know *what*. It has grasped, if not the answers, then at least the issues that will dominate the coming debates. We've already touched on two of these issues: in the first place, the importance of the political and cultural background as a codeterminant of the development and the stability of democracy; in the second place, the relation between nation and civil society (a relation that describes problems that could become more important for Eastern Europe than for a Germany that has well integrated itself into Europe). Both cases ultimately concern the status of formal institutions under the rule of law. We've already discussed the problems of a coming global domestic policy and the role of a united Germany in the transformed constellation of world powers in the context of the Gulf War. Perhaps the most important issues we face are the urgent transitional problems arising from the unprecedented systemic changeover from state socialism to a market economy. The 'remedial revolution'[10] throws no new light on our *old* problems – but they nevertheless now stand in the light of a changed situation.

In fact, it's the conservative intellectuals who forced their old interpretations onto the changed situation in 1990, so that, for example, a Heideggerian could discover in the 'madness, madness' of 9 November that *Kairos* that the master himself had missed in 1933. There was the neo-Aristotelian who saw the nation-state as the fulfillment of that dream of a substantive ethical life, a dream that he had always held up against the nightmare of abstract constitutional patriotism. Or the leading expert of German idealism who understands contemporary events as just so many references to that German Republic that the best among us had already grasped – futilely, in the medium of thought – at the opening of the nineteenth century. Or the historian who hurried to Wartburg on invitation from the German Dueling Society, determined to bridge the gap from 1817 to the present simply as a way of freeing the grandfathers from the stigma of the German 'special path' [*Sonderweg*].

This is the same path taken by the political historian (who prefers to be introduced by the conservative feuilleton as a Social Democrat by marriage) to win the lost battles of yesteryear. Her article (from the FAZ of 12 December 1990) expresses the need to rewrite the history of the Federal Republic. Even though this republic owes its comparatively liberal climate to the broad change of attitudes set in motion by the student revolt of 1968, here's how the commentary of the generation of '68ers now reads: 'The intellectual experience of the divided Germany entered into an unholy alliance with the emotional experience of prosperity. The arrogance that arose from this alliance played a dirty trick on the '68ers – or those of them who survived politically – by preventing them from recognizing the signs of the times. History outfoxed them – and voted them out. . . . Their legacy will not be carried on. It has sunk out of view, opening up the vista – of that younger generation molded by the experiences of 1989 and 1990.' Antje Vollmer, in her gentle way, has shifted the accents of this argument enough to show why political biographies can't be written so simply according to dates of birth. She takes good advantage of the Bonn experiences and Biermann's[11] interpretation of Daedelus and Icarus when she instead distinguishes between those types with staying power and those who have actually broken down. There may well be this kind of generational arithmetic, according to which the grandfathers and the grandchildren enter into a coalition because both, in the heat of the moment, find themselves aligned against the black-sheep middle generation. But it's more likely to add up this way in the feuilletons than in reality.

» «

In this context, we could also think back to the so-called Liter-ature Controversy that was touched off by Christa Wolf and her short autobiography in the summer of 1990. Wasn't that a genuine generational problem?[12]

» «

That's right. My generation got and took full advantage of all the opportunities after the war. It dominated the intel-lectual scene for an abnormally long time, no differently in philosophy departments than in literature. A lack of talent in the younger generation wasn't the cause of this: when their turn came, the intellectuals who came up immediately after my generation saw in the historical situation no rea-son to rebel against their immediate predecessors and pro-claim a new beginning. If that is what's happening now, it's quite natural. What's absurd is *how* it's happening. The writers who came to prominence in the first decades after the war are now accused of practicing an 'aesthetics of con-viction' and are dismissed as 'pillars of the state.' Literature usually gets driven out and replaced by literature – now the literary critics want to take care of this all by themselves.

The literature debate surrounding Christa Wolf was also a good example of how repetitive these sandbox games really are – after the Wall came down, the same feuilleton[13] that had worked for decades to rehabilitate our young con-servative 'spokesmen of the *Reich*' hurried to make good on Peter Rühmkorf's[14] expectation that 'now socialism will have to do what the Nazis never did: really pay for what it did.' But the subtext of the whole Literature Controversy is of an even older style. There was a sense that the intellectuals of the West and the East were finally being brought up on the charge of their dangerously irresponsible utopianism and would be exposed as the true enemies of the people. Ivan Nagel[15] is exactly right in understanding this as 'pest control': 'The new view being taken of the writers of the GDR and the Federal Republic is understandable as a practical action: two swarms of (blow)flies with one swat' (*Süddeutsche Zeitung*, 22–23 December 1990).

»«

But apart from the intellectuals, we have plenty of reminders in Germany these days of the first years of the Federal Republic, when the politics of reconstruction of Konrad Adenauer and Ludwig Erhard effectively prevented any clean break with the ideologies of the past. Instead, the past was repressed – and its ruins are still to be seen today. It seems that the climate of public opinion emerging from Kohl's Deutschlandpolitik of the 1990s is reverting to this older pattern.

»«

In his analysis of the first elections in the united Germany, the Freiburg political scientist Dieter Oberndörfer came to the conclusion that the emerging picture of how the shares of votes of the major political parties divide up is astonishingly similar to what it was in the 1950s. This naturally holds true for aggregate quantities, and not the underlying structures, which look entirely different. It's the same all over: a deceptive sort of déjà vu begins to generate historical effects. The 'Wessis' have such an allergic reaction to the peculiar habits and mental traits of their brothers and sisters from the East because they recognize themselves in them. Images of their own early years rise up, years when the German petty virtues emerged from their political costume party – in which a lot of people were dressed in brown – and deflected themselves into the historyless private sphere. Images from that time, when national pride migrated wordlessly into pride in the economy, reappeared in November 1989. Ever since, they have monopolized that collective power of imagination whose flexibility and creativity are essential for dealing with the problems of the future. It's certainly true that precisely the utter newness of this transition from bankrupted state socialism to developed capitalism can serve as an explanation for this regressive tendency. The first generation that took to the skies in the earliest propeller-driven aircraft, learning to navigate the uncertainties of a new element, came to interpret their experiences of air travel in terms that were borrowed from the old vocabulary of sea voyaging. It's the magic of words in the taming of unknown risks. For me, the invocation of the model of currency reform brought 1948 back to mind – a plan that was implemented under completely different conditions and wasn't much use as a model.[16] Think of the political ads of Ludwig Erhard with his dachshund that the administration spokesman Klein had made up for the *Volkskammer* election campaign: *The Past as Future*. Naturally, the 1990s aren't the 1950s. But the temptation to choose models from the past for the interpretation of the future seems impossible to resist. The futurity of the past could have been worked through with a self-aware creation of a constitution. Instead, the future is being perceived in the form of the past: 'Let's get it over with, just like we did once before!'

» «

Looking back on the difficult history of the Germans might lead one to ask if a society is ever capable of 'managing' its own past. Or if history doesn't repeat itself after all. Is there really something like a collective repetition compulsion?

» «

Once upon a time, 'original sin' was the theological term for what we now refer to as repetition compulsion, whether on the individual or the collective level. Ralph Giordiano has called this (impressively documented) repression of the Nazi past – the very sociopsychological basis for the reconstructive triumphs of Adenauer and Erhard that we just spoke of – a 'second guilt.' Sophinette Becker and Hans Becker are now warning of a 'third guilt.' In a very enlightening article (*Frankfurter Rundschau,* 9 November 1990), the two psychologists read the discussions over the Stasi past as a latent discourse about the Nazi past:

> The current discussion in the former GDR on the period between 1945 and 1989 often has the effect of a caricature of the situation in West Germany after 1945: everybody was a victim of the system; everybody was betrayed; apart from a small group of big shots, nobody benefited from the system, etc., etc. For the most part, a real confrontation with one's own participation never took place; people concentrated on their own sorrows instead. One enormous difference, of course, stands out: the lynching mood; the merciless persecution of scapegoats from the toppled leadership ranks of the former GDR, something that never happened to the Nazis after 1945.

This lynching mood acts as the complement to the demands for a clean break with the past: 'The majority are asking for politicians who approve both of an immediate

amnesty law and also of a vigorous prosecution of the supposedly guilty parties – two demands that only apparently
contradict one another.'

I'm no psychologist. I also know how difficult it is to
verify statements about the motives and defensive strategies of large groups. But Becker and Becker's sociopsychological analysis is highly illuminating in the context of the
history of German mentalities. A good deal of the reactions
both here and in the East can be understood as the activa-
tion of a resentment deeply rooted in the history of the
Third Reich and World War II. At first glance, one might
regard the party preferences that have developed in the new
states as 'rational,' in the sense of enlightened self-interest.
But one should also not completely discount the kinds
of psychohistorical observations that, for example, Jurek
Becher has made of Germans in the East, where, as he has
observed,

> the Stalinist occupation forces of the Soviet Union were
> able to pick up where the Nazis had left off. . . . I would
> venture to say that the pressure for adaptation was expe-
> rienced far more harshly by most of the citizens of the
> GDR than was the case in the Third Reich, and I suspect
> that the identification between the native residents and
> the Nazi state was far greater than what it was later in the
> GDR. I cannot imagine that under free elections, even im-
> mediately after the war, the NSDAP would have received a
> rebuff similar to the recent rejection of the SED. If one
> compares the sheer mass of refusal of the party, indeed the
> hatred that expressed itself after the *Wende,* with the re-
> bellion that came of forty years of the GDR, one establishes
> a certain lack of symmetry. (*Die Zeit,* 3 August 1990)

In light of this sort of reaction, the talk of a 'collective repetition compulsion' seems to me not entirely un-founded. With more specific reference to the ruling elites of the SED, Lutz Niemann's recently published autobiographical investigations (in *Prokla* 80 [1990]: 40–70) lend further support to the hypothesis that the peculiar willingness for subordination characteristic of the generation that moved through the party ranks and took over leadership roles beginning in the early 1960s – the HJ/FDJ generation, corresponding to the second 'reconstruction' generation in the West – can only be explained psychologically, as a symbiosis with the old-guard communists of the early days of the GDR.

» «

Since the Wall came down, repeated attempts have been made to open a political dialogue between East and West. Each attempt has run into the difficulty that, over the course of the last forty years, two truly different systems have been formed, each with its own language, its own models for socialization, and its own convictions about justice. No dialogue working toward mutual understanding is happening. Political communication is becoming distorted. How can communication be rescued from this distortion? What issues could form something like a national consensus in the new Germany?

» «

What you're calling distorted political communication appears as a cartoon image on the talk show circuit: the Wessis, with a monopoly on morality, in a face-to-face confrontation with the humiliated and 'dismantled' Ossis, who struggle – nobly – for their self-respect. The weaker are the more sensitive. While life barely altered its old rhythm in the West, in Berlin both sides of this face-to-face are now rubbing each other raw. Body language alone is enough for us to recognize the utter moral impoverishment that the hurry-up tempo of the unification process has left us. A certain distance is lacking. An encounter that assumes the autonomy of both sides would require that first each side clear up its own separate history of forty years of the FRG and GDR, and that each side win a self-understanding of its own.

At the moment, an entirely different development seems to be in the wings. The more powerful Federal Republic is on the brink of dragging the struggle over *its* history out into the open – a struggle that, after unification, some have begun in brashly revanchist spirit – while the history of the GDR is being more or less silently buried, and bequeathed to the next generation as a skeleton in the closet. Since the Gulf War, the motto of this sad state of affairs has become: 'We must become a normal people again.' But a bisected history and the collective self-understanding of victors would be a fragile foundation for a durable national consensus. The changed world situation itself will make the unified Germany a new nation. It will have to depend on just such a consensus in the increasingly bitter controversies over domestic policy.

There has to be a consensus over the future role of Germany in Europe, and over the sort of role of assistance that Germany, as the economic locomotive of the European Community, is to assume for a peaceful social and economic development within Eastern Europe. Further, I would wish for a consensus on a constitutional patriotism deeply rooted in the experiences of German history. Among these experiences, for example (as H. A. Winckler[17] reminds us in *Die Zeit*, 28 September 1990), is the fact that since the 1870s the concept of 'nationalism' has undergone a metamorphosis from a left-wing to a right-wing rallying cry; also, naturally, the reminder that Germany is the only highly industrialized country in which an economic crisis led a democratic state under the rule of law to collapse into a fascist dictatorship. Further, we need to get clear on the formal and functional transformations of the nation-state, without immediately exposing ourselves to the criticism of the 'arrogance of postnationalism.' Finally, we need to mark out the terrain on which the struggle to make good on the universally shared lip service about the social and ecological domestication of capitalism will be fought. How we're going to handle the mass immigrations from the East and from the exploited countries of the Third World is going to be decided only in the electoral contests of individual politicians. We have to know what it is that we want to defend: the crude economic chauvinism of a society as divided on the inside as it is walled off from the outside world? or the integrity of a highly individualized society – a society that of course has to keep its damageable functional system intact, but only for the sake of implementing the demands of its universalistic constitutional principles?

Further, I'm not convinced that in the third millennium basic political agreements, which must be very abstract in order not to endanger pluralism, will have to be expressed in symbols. The flags behind the governmental desks were copied from the USA. But there, political socialization, which in any case keeps alive ideas from the enlightened eighteenth century, forms the most important level of the social integration of an enormous continent.

Here in Germany, though, the administration's attempts to rally the people to the red, black, and gold smacks of manipulation. It's just as artificial as the passionate debates over the capital city. Personally, I agree with my colleague Lepsius, who says that we neither have nor need a metropolis: 'We are a universal-provincial country.' There may well be a lot of good reasons for making Berlin the seat of government. But the worst reason is spatially congealed 'spirit.' In the high-minded nagging against antimetropolitan resentment, against the proliferation of the provincials, against apolitical hedonism, flight from world politics, and so on, I can recognize only the young conservative's confusion of intellectual productivity and the allure of power. Please – what's the point today of the 'aura of the state' for intellectuals who just maybe have outgrown the Carl Schmittian cast of mind?

Europe's Second Chance

MICHAEL HALLER: *Let's now turn to the consequences of the demise of state socialism for Europe. What will become of Eastern European societies? How will Western European societies react? The irreversible bankruptcy of state socialism was something that none of us had reckoned with concretely. When the GDR was still in existence, we dealt with it in a very restrained manner – we intellectuals as well as the liberal mass media. Most of the criticism of the GDR that was expressed at all came accompanied with the mention of mitigating circumstances of one kind or another; reports of the totalitarian features of the state apparatus that expelled artists carried out of the GDR had little resonance here. And yet hardly one of the Western intellectuals held the GDR in high esteem. In the undogmatic leftist circles, it had long been agreed that conditions in the GDR were not really what one would call 'socialist.' In hindsight, how do we explain this peculiar ambivalence in relations with the former GDR?*

» «

JÜRGEN HABERMAS: You're asking *me*? Those who grew up in West Germany after the war – that is, vis-à-vis the GDR – couldn't harbor any illusions about the repressive conditions in the satellites of the Soviet Union. Those of us who turned to socialism under the intellectual influence of Western Marxism understood ourselves not through but precisely despite this 'real existing socialism.' This is how I answered a similar question in Israel in 1977. Of course I always had reservations about strengthening the anticommunist choir, which with us in the West was so predomi-

73

nant. But I never left any doubt about my own refusal of Stalinism and my assessment of Soviet Marxism – just as little as Horkheimer or Adorno. In this sense there can be no talk of 'ambivalence.' Given the political socialization of my generation in the late 1940s and early 1950s, this is no great achievement. I didn't stand on the barricades as a Maoist in 1968 either, as did many of the new philosophers who thought at that time to order *tout le monde* into bidding farewell to the 'master thinkers.' Life histories are different. There are no representative individuals.

» «

Our discussion has already touched on the false claim of real existing socialism in Eastern Europe, namely that it oriented itself according to the model of a just and peaceful society. Was it this claim that caused West European intellectuals to don such ideological blinkers in their attitudes toward the United States?

» «

I opposed the Vietnam War from the same motives and convictions as those of my students at the New School in New York in 1967–68, who besieged the local induction center every morning at 6 A.M., and who one by one disappeared toward Canada in order to escape military service. The American government's intervention in a civil war that stood in the context of decolonialization was hardly true to the values claimed in its own constitution. These were the same principles that I identified with after the war. As with many of my generation, the encounter with the political traditions of this country, with a genuine American heritage, from Thomas Paine to pragmatism, left deep traces behind.

» «

Was there a period in your life when you believed – or hoped – that Eastern Europe would take the path of democratic social-ism and one day would triumph over the capitalist West, at least morally, if not also economically?

»«

I've certainly represented more orthodox positions than I do today. One makes an effort to learn. But I never needed to learn that the dream of 'catching up and overtaking' was absurd.[1] I was always convinced that if things are to 'go forward' at all, they have to go forward where productive forces and legal democracy are the furthest developed, and that's in the West. My leftist friends have made this 'Euro-centrism' into an accusation. And today it's not without sympathy that I observe that world history has offered a unified Europe a second chance. We've watched the rise and fall of the great empires over the centuries – the Ro-mans and the Carolingians, the Portugese and the Span-iards, the English and the French, the Russians and – it now virtually appears – the Americans. Not one of these empires appeared on the world stage a second time. Today, however, that force that Max Weber attributed to Western rationality could once again be gathering – and this time, I hope, free of all imperialistic ambitions and with so little narcissistic self-absorption that a Europe that has learned from its own history can help other countries emerge from *their* nine-teenth centuries.

I don't want to sidestep your question. Naturally, I've had hopes – more during the Prague Spring, less during the Brezhnev era – that one day bureaucratic socialism might have liberalized itself and taken a learning step, one that could have served as the functional equivalent of the state-social compromise of the West. Had that occurred, the advantages and disadvantages specific to each system could have been matched up in a complementary kind of opposition (although at a lower stage of development, of course) – to oversimplify a bit: the development of forces of production and innovation on the one side, greater social security and (where possible) qualitatively directed growth on the other. That hope is now abandoned.

» «

Did you ever regard the system of the SED *as reformable? Could the* GDR *have constructed a popular democratic socialism – democratic in the sense of the representation of interests through a plurality of political parties tailored according to the Western model; socialist in the sense of a social power of access to the basic means of production?*

» «

In *The Remedial Revolution* (1990) I reprinted an interview that I gave for *Sinn und Form* in 1988. In it, I expressed the hope that the policy of *perestroika* would finally break through the Honecker regime and thus would also lead to a pluralization of the political system in the GDR. I saw then, and still see now, nothing that refutes in advance the possibility of a democratic potential within a self-revolutionizing state socialism. With the opening of the Wall, however, all the dams have burst. I say this with no regrets.

» «

Once again: Marxism-Leninism failed to introduce and install socialism as a dirigistic *political system. What are the consequences of this failure for the Western world, and in particular for us in Germany?*

» «

I can't really offer a response beyond what comes to mind to a halfway-informed newspaper reader. Over the medium term, capitalism will open up new markets in the Second World. The cluster of nations with state-run economies had long since grown dependent on world markets, but now Western modes of production are penetrating the interior of cultures and ways of life that themselves were already being undermined and hollowed out in their traditional substances by deeply entrenched bureaucratic modernization processes. It's hard to say how this second, equally reckless modernization process will look when seen up close. In any case, the West will have to think up a new type of developmental aid program for those countries able to create tolerable conditions for the introduction of capital and know-how. Defense policies have also entered into a new era as a result of the dissolution of the Western and Soviet blocs. Rearmament and disarmament place the military-industrial complex under pressure; for us, they will also lead to the important consequence of a restructuring both of federal budgets and of important sectors of the global economy. I'm hoping that these long-term trends are being only temporarily overshadowed by the Gulf War.

New international alliances have already taken shape. In terms of world domestic policy, a lot of new room for action has been opened up, as the UN resolutions on Kuwait show. We shouldn't be misled by the Gulf War: with the deconstruction of bipolar tensions it's becoming increasingly clear that the one remaining superpower has really very few conflicts under control. The developing disparities in the global economy, the failures of the World Bank's developmental programs, the uncontrolled spread of nuclear weapons, the emigration pressures from the mobile populations of underdeveloped countries who have been uprooted from their traditional cultures, all come together to form a mixture as explosive as it is unpredictable. It demands a more broadly effective network of global planning, as well as a more neutral and efficient international policing force. We've already discussed this. Satisfying these demands will initially produce a broader gap between, on the one hand, the necessities of a social and economic redevelopment of those regions of the world for which Calcutta, Cairo, and Lima are the sad symbols and, on the other hand, the fixed ecological limitations of an overtaxed natural environment.

The immediate consequences for Germany and for Western Europe are clear. The challenge facing German domestic developmental policies – raising the standard of living conditions in the former East Germany as quickly as possible and stemming the flow of East-West emigration – now stands under other premises for the relations between Western and Eastern Europe. The statisticians are now working with figures of between twenty million and thirty million emigrants from Eastern to Western Europe. This enormous flood of emigration represents an entirely new kind of economic sanction, and the West will be able to cope with it only by formulating an economic development policy for the Second World of unprecedented scale. This is the factual flip side of the West's normative duty to respond to the collapse of the Soviet empire. Since the lifting of the Iron Curtain, the destinies of Eurasian societies and cultures have become more closely intertwined than ever before. And never before has the weight of responsibility for the anomie, civil war, and chaos breaking out across the reaches of the East fallen so unequivocally on Western shoulders.

The horrifying magnitude of these problems relativizes

the specifically German concerns that we've discussed up until now. I think that the pressure from without is going to force the Germans out of their narcissistic preoccupation with their own comparatively small problems. The scale of relevance is going to shift; a circumstance that supports the expectation that the intellectual fronts of the postwar period are becoming obsolete, and that we are going to be arguing within another coordinate system, that we'll have to find entirely new interpretations for an unexpected situation. German problems are becoming less German.

» «

The logic of deterrence generated by the East-West confrontation was not only perilous, it was also anachronistic. But in political terms, this logic also had another, less unambiguous dimension to it: the contest between the two systems could be understood as a competition that would act as a spur to development in the industrialized societies. Some theoreticians hold that were it not for this competitive pressure, the social components of our market society would be as weakly developed today as they are in the United States. Has the dismantling of the East-West opposition and the world dominance of capitalist market economies forced our societies to forfeit this dynamic?

» «

The ever-popular Fukuyama question.[2] I have to confess that I don't think much of these diagnoses of the end of history. In his most recent book, the clever Baudrillard has once again risen painfully to the defense of history at a standstill – the vision of some huge bell jar under which all historical options have frozen up. In point of fact, the administered world really has reached the point of collapse. Anyway, Baudrillard has only been able to capture the attention of those with short memories. I already read most of this in Arnold Gehlen when I was a student. Neither version of this supposedly alternativeless course of world history – whether as the result of the labors of disappointment of right-wing intellectuals or as the smug triumphalism of self-satisfied liberals – has much to recommend it. As history goes over into another aggregate state, things get hotter, not colder.

Until now, occidental rationality has generated all of its alternatives from out of itself. This is no different today. At the same time, while it promotes the homogenizing dissemination of a global industrial culture, occidental rationality also generates from itself a new pluralization of forms of life, a new individualization of lifestyles, and a multicultural diversity extending to new and entrenched forms of fundamentalism. It is confronted with challenges of an entirely new sort from the outside. In this regard, I don't share the optimistic idea that, now that the false alternative of socialism is out of the way, the path is clear for an even faster process of the domestication of capitalism to the point of unrecognizability – as if, in the shadows of weakened system imperatives, the ability to divert attention from one's own deficiencies serves to clear away the barriers from a path that we were always meaning to take anyway. I believe that we are faced with very risky new tasks: the historical and philosophical faith that the World Spirit only poses itself tasks that it can accomplish is passé. Things are going to get much more tense, but for that reason also much more intellectually exciting. I say this, of course, without any enthusiasm for the heroic nihilism of the pensioned soldiers of the global civil war – the post-structuralists, who strike me occasionally as the last of the foreign legionnaires discharged from the ranks of the international class struggle. I rather share Christian Meier's[3] impression of the 'exhaustion of previously held orientations.' He proposes that there is hardly any prospect for this posthistorical retirement home where, according to Odo Marquand, 'nothing happens anymore and, insofar as they aren't "immobilized," everyone is excited.'

In the same issue of *Merkur* (October/November 1990), Ernst-Otto Czempiel has an analysis of the changed international scene that illuminates one new challenge very well. The organizational form of the nation-state, indeed the entity of the territorial state as such, is just as washed up as the whole conception of the political as determined through the primacy of the guarantee of order – the Hobbesian concept that the political is a function of the inner and outer stabilization of authority. The European world of states that formed in 1648 has long since sunk out of view. But the constellation of state, economy, and society that developed after the Peace of Westphalia still maintained itself through the period of world wars. This period is now over, and this constellation is no longer adequate to the complexity of the new situation, a fact that is clear enough from a glance at the condition of an empire that still maintains the second largest potential for military destruction in the world, but nevertheless has forfeited its own room for action. Fortunately, the Soviet Union no longer appears to be in any position to turn its internal conflicts outward in the classic manner; in any event, we'd better hope so. Before the Gulf War, Czempiel sketched out a scenario that even afterward has not proved to be entirely false:

The architecture of world politics is no longer the old one; the world is no longer a world of *states,* in which possession of the means of military force is the key to the distribution of power and influence. Nor is it yet a world society that denies itself such means, transferring them instead to some central authority. This new world is closest to what one could call a *social* world: one made up of various state organizations but determined by the interests of different societies.

He maintains that 'the socioeconomic advancement of society is to be had only at the price of decreased domination: this lesson is being learned all over the world, and not just in a positive sense.'

Again, Marx and Saint-Simon stand unmistakably in the background of tendencies of societies of our type. Of course, we would be overlooking the contemporary relevance of this diagnosis entirely if we were to explain the preeminence of the problems of prosperity over those of securing military power in such societies solely from a system-theoretical perspective. 'Society' changes its position simultaneously in relation both to state and economy: in the political public sphere, society demands action from both sides, not only in the categories of prosperity and subjective freedom, but also in the categories of justice and political participation. It's better to formulate this normatively: society is to constitute itself precisely as a 'civil society,' in a framework constructed from the radicalized freedom of political communication. This would demand a shifting of the division of the forces of social integration between money and administrative power on the one side, and solidarity on the other side. This view of a 'depoliticization' of state administration, in favor of a civil society capable of making the economy more sensitive to its external costs, produces a perspective on the future of *perestroika,* which has become just as necessary for the West as for the Soviet Union. The organizational forms of the modern state system, geared to military security and the stabilization of authority, have fallen into decay. This is true despite the Gulf War.

» «

Eastern European society, particularly in the industrialized states of Poland, Hungary, and Czechoslovakia, appears to be particularly degraded. As we speak, the systemic changes there are contributing to the rise of essentially conservative groups, which have spoken out in favor of the model of the authoritarian caretaker state, a model in which the state is to minimize direct intervention in the economy and instead merely assist in the development of undirected capitalism. Critics of this model maintain that Western Europe will soon constitute the socially advanced side of Europe, while the former socialist countries will make up Europe's most backward countries. Is this a grotesque characterization?

» «

Now, these countries you name at least have their memories of a brief republican period between the wars, and of an economic and cultural place in the old Europe of the pre-war era. In the Soviet Union, on the other hand, the cumulative effects of more than seventy years of real socialism establish a very different point of departure. But all of these countries, as well as Yugoslavia, Romania, and Bulgaria, are faced with the alternative of a regression into *other* pasts: into nationalism and anti-Semitism, into all the ethnocentric fantasies that rise from the Hades of the nineteenth century and that represent familiar (and understandable) social and psychological dams for the suppression of aggressions in acutely depressed periods. For the Slavic countries, the *mene tekel* 'The Past as Future' has a very obvious significance. That Western Europe itself hasn't succumbed to the pull of these negative currents is more out of luck than merit.

» «

What is your view of the transformation currently going on in the Eastern European countries: will the transition to democracy be successful?

» «

The transition from state socialism to a technically highly developed, electronically interconnected global capitalism is without precedent. I'm no expert on central and Eastern European development. But we can't close our eyes to the facts that brought socialism into being in the first place – not only in the form of an effective capitalist self-criticism, but also in the form of an alternative program of development. The Western world isn't made up solely of its North Atlantic vanguard, but also of South America, of sub-Saharan Africa, South Africa, India, and Southeast Asia. Despite the democratic transitions we've seen over the past decade in the Philippines, or in Namibia, Chile, Argentina, and Nicaragua, the evidence continues to mount that there is no automatic relationship between capitalist modernization and political freedom. In countries with no adequate equivalent for what Max Weber correctly emphasized as the cultural peripheral conditions for European modernity, capitalist developmental poverty, ecological devastation, political repression, and cultural disintegration braid together into an increasingly desperate feedback loop. Developmental policies have produced still another vicious circle. The experience of the failures of old-fashioned developmental aid programs has served as a reason, and pretext, for the increasing unwillingness to continue the export of capital into developing countries. But one mustn't look only to the barbarian living conditions to see where modernization brings neither prosperity nor freedom.

In perhaps his most beautiful book, *Natural Law and Human Dignity,* Ernst Bloch established an important distinction between two very different dimensions: social utopias depict conditions in which the lot of the 'overworked and overburdened' is improved; natural law, on the other hand, constructs conditions in which the 'degraded and insulted' can once again hold their heads up.[4] Progress in one dimension doesn't have to correlate with progress in the other. India offers the largest example of a decades-old competitive democracy spread out across the breadth of an entire subcontinent, yet still unable to contribute anything toward the redress of the kind of conditions that so horrified Günter Grass in Calcutta. At the same time, the conflict in Kuwait reminds us of the oil-rich sheikdoms of the Middle East, whose modern economies persist in essentially feudal political conditions. Even examples of successful capitalist development – South Korea, Taiwan, or perhaps the Philippines – show how hard it is to find an economy prospering under stable democratic conditions.

So it's hard to say whether Eastern Europe will be capable of a democratic transition to capitalist prosperity. Will these countries – in which the population was accustomed to a relatively low level of social security – be able to make it through the coming period of delayed satisfaction of needs, of growing social inequity, mass unemployment, thwarted ambitions, and disappointing lives, without once again endangering the newly achieved institutions of freedom? Will the population sit still until the Walesas have learned from the Michniks?[5] Provided that whatever capital that was generated by the state socialist system isn't squandered, at least these countries won't need to make up for the initial phases of capital accumulation – the problem of the Trust Company in the former East Germany.[6]

The former East Bloc nations have other advantages compared to countries such as Brazil, Argentina, or Chile: relatively mild disparity of incomes; an old, stable, and well-qualified workforce; the egalitarian value orientations of the masses; and so forth. But the more democratic the framework is, the harder it is to carry out the kind of so-cially and economically painful reform programs that are demanded by the deconstruction of the systems of social benefits and subsidies, monopolistic state industries, the stranglehold of the managerial elites, and so on. Demo-cratic conditions enhance the chances for the successful resistance and opposition of those who have the most to lose. Adam Przeworski[7] has enumerated the threats to countries such as Poland, Hungary, and Yugoslavia:

> The organization of the state is weak, the economy is too protected and controlled by monopolistic enterprises, the bureaucracy bloated . . . agricultural production is inefficient, political parties and other such organizations are decrepit. Governments that are able to grow in these kinds of conditions are prey to a host of ills: to political and economic pressures from large corporations; from populist movements with dubious loyalty to democracy; from militaries that stand threateningly in the wings, holding themselves in readiness; from church hierarchies that waffle between authoritarianism and commitment to social justice; from nationalist voices that veer into xeno-phobic violence. (*Transit* 1 [1990]: 206)

Visiting Eastern European capitals and talking with leading figures in culture and politics, one often hears the complaint that the Eastern European intellectual class is extremely small. Clearly, a middle class that would serve as a kind of intellectual resource comparable to our own is missing. The argument here is that the Eastern European countries will have to reconstruct a middle class before they can install a functional equivalent for the Western European–style system of bourgeois civil society. Is middle Europe undergoing a sort of remedial process, in order to make all the new contacts and connections that will be necessary for this?

» «

Well, the 'remedial process' is certainly highly relevant for what the elites want just as much as the masses: to set about achieving the degree of prosperity, social security, and political freedom that has been achieved in the West. What one could call the reconstruction of bourgeois society plays an important role in this. But what precisely does 'bourgeois society' mean? Especially if one looks beyond the particular situation in the divided Germany, there was indeed an intellectual class. And a restoration of the prewar bourgeoisie is probably neither possible nor desirable. 'Bourgeois' or 'civil' society has become a key concept of political self-understanding for the dissidents in Eastern Europe – and, as I've said, also a key term for their radical democratic fellows in the West – because specific experiences of *loss* are articulated in it. And of success, during the liberalization process. Indeed, once one refrains from making normative judgments, one can conceive of state socialism as an inflationary overburdening of administrative power. In this kind of society, the mechanisms of bureaucratic rule have not only destroyed the resistance of an economic process

87

that is decentrally steered through markets, but also the *communicative rationality of the life world* – they have shattered the very logic of public and private conditions for mutual understanding; they have devastated the areas of cultural reproduction, social integration and even socialization itself. There's nothing evil about administrative power considered in itself. But it demands that functions be filled, that other resources of social integration be replaced, which can't be filled or substituted in this way without producing pathologies.

Elemer Hankiss[8] (in an anthology edited by MacLean, Montefiori, and Winch, *The Political Responsibility of Intellectuals* [Cambridge: Cambridge University Press, 1990], 29ff.), has described one such pathology as the systematic 'loss of the sense of responsibility.' His analysis leads to the heart of what you touched on earlier in our discussion of the destruction and reconstruction of bourgeois society. I don't think we really have any idea of the sheer scale of the destruction that administrative intervention and supervision wreaked on the moral infrastructure of everyday life in the former GDR, among families and friends, in communities and neighborhoods, schools, in the workplace, and so on. The devastation of informal relationships, social groups, associations, and networks; the dissolution of social identities; the calculated indoctrination of new values; the erosion of accepted behavioral norms; a crippling of initiative and personal independence that extends even into regions of activity that are beyond direct surveillance (regions that are as overregulated as they are underlegislated); isolation and the sealing off of outlets for spontaneous public communication – these are some of the categories that Hankiss uses to analyze the social-structural conditions for a withdrawal from possibilities, motivations, and capacities for *responsible* decisions among options with foreseeable consequences. It is against this background that one has to understand the revaluation of 'civil society' that has risen to the status of an alternative concept in the discussions of Eastern European intellectuals.

During the first phase of liberalization, countless autonomous groups, unions, circles, clubs, bands, and organizations rose from the ashes the moment that the control of the state bureaucracies was loosened – groups that defined themselves in opposition to the state; that is, as 'society.' This changed the meaning of the concept of 'bourgeois society' as Marx had inherited it from Hegel. But the semantics are less important than the reality. The question is whether and for how long this newly emerged political public sphere, institutionally shored up with the new structure of citizens' movements, will be able to survive the collapse of the totalitarian regime. In the GDR, the New Forum offered a good example, understanding itself as a social movement and having no desire to take the last step to becoming a full-fledged political party. Also, the failure of this attempt illustrates that in the GDR – for the time being – the past rules over the future.

» «

Let's take that as the occasion to focus our discussion more on Western society. One could think of the radical democratic grass-roots organizations that emerged in the 1970s as the counterimage to the concept of the state in the East. For those grass-roots organizations, reason was to operate not in the state apparatus but rather through the commitment of citizens, articulating their own wills and practicing solidarity in order to have an effect on the political system. A breath of the dialectic passed through our political lives.

Radical democratic theory in the West was inspired by the semantic shift within the concept of 'civil society' that took place in the political self-understanding of dissidents. But again one must be careful to distinguish between the realities of West and East. In Eastern Europe, I'm afraid, the structures of civil society are so completely the mirror image of the panoptic state apparatus that, while they do emerge during the first stages of the state's decay, they also disappear along with it – initially, at any rate. In Western societies, the new social movements have an entirely different basis. They proceed according to other motives, stand in a different context, and have different goals, simply because the measure of liberality that people in the East are struggling for is already met here. These differences become very visible – as in a test tube – when civil jurists and the Greens in the GDR meet together with the 'Greens' in the Federal Republic.

» «

At the beginning of the 1980s, the grass-roots alternative movements linked up to form the Green party. From then on, the Greens operated as a part of the political system, even while trying to circumvent the rules of this very system. Today, at the beginning of the 1990s, these rules are proving to be far too rigid, and the grass-roots experiment is widely regarded as a failure. What significance do you attach to this failure?

» «

First of all, one has to understand that the 'Greens' nationwide were only as successful as their oppositional status permitted them to be. It followed through on one of its two major issues – the ecology – at least politically. The other issue, peace and disarmament, was up until the outbreak of the Gulf War pushed more or less into the background by

the new world constellation – MBB must rearm and disarm.[9]
The Greens weren't able to put a stop to criminal arms ex-
portations, of course. But they gave a new impetus to femi-
nism – also in the political classes themselves. In the end,
they had what one could call a style-forming effect in political service and in parliament. They forcefully widened the
margins of tolerance. Think back, for example, to the prud-
ish notions of 'constitutional loyalty' that were the standard
fare back in the 1970s, and that so quickly became something no one could manage. Most of all, the Greens transformed political procedures, room for participation, an unorthodox mobility, the culture of dispute in the public
sphere. Who would have thought it possible that a party
that came off as quarrelsome and chaotic as the Greens
would contrive to gain sympathies and votes for years
among the well-behaved burghers of Germany? Their
greatest service was that they *didn't* reproduce the old pattern of leftist populism, because the politics they practiced
was oriented not so much by public mood as it was by public discourse. Even a chaotic discourse is always essentially
more democratic than an affect provoked and solidified
with ads and demagoguery. When all is said and done, the
Greens were and still are a civilizing force. I sing this song
of praise even though I never voted for the Greens: I've
always been a bit uneasy with the leftist-nationalist fringes
and the leftovers from the old cadres. But in hindsight I
suppose this is the product of a kind of Social Democratic
overcautiousness. Besides, one can't blame the Greens if
there was never the acid test of a Red-Green coalition on the
federal level. The somewhat regressive domestic counter-
effects of the administration's unification process, which
we've already spoken of, hit the Greens just as hard as the
SPD, itself now split between Lafontaine and Rappe.

In brief, one can speak of the failure of the experiment of grass-roots democracy only if one regards it too concret-istically, as some Greens do themselves. The New Social Movements indeed no longer belong to the type of mass movement that occupied the streets – and the dreams of the revolutionary theorists – in the nineteenth and twentieth centuries. The traditional models were the general strike on the one hand, the uninformed fascist mob on the other. The further that mass civilization progresses, the more this romanticism of mass action fades – despite Leipzig and Wenzelplatz.[10] This has nothing to do with raw numbers. The human chain more than one hundred kilometers long, the elated mass demonstrations of 1983 in Bonn and else-where, and later the enormous peace demonstration in the *Hofgarten* in Bonn after the outbreak of the Gulf War were a living denial of the belief in violence, of the vision of the active masses fused into some subject writ large. This is naturally regarded from the old republican point of view. The demonstrations in which the outrage at social poverty in the GDR speaks out belongs rather to the traditional type (as in the PDS and union slogans, which channeled the rage).[11] Nevertheless, the belief in the subject in large for-mat, like the belief in direct access to the great system, is, thank God, washed up.

The New Social Movements have themselves become the motor for processes of pluralization and individualization. They represent an abstractive process that our conception of democracy must now follow, if it is to remain realistic. The mass dynamic of the streams of public communica-tion, and not the psychology of the masses, is the vehicle for the realization of democratic participation and the de-velopment of a true pluralism. Only through public communication can the institutions of freedom be filled with the substance of a rational process of the formation of political views and political will.

» «

Both the end of real, existing socialism and the defeat of alternative groups have contributed to a greatly diminished interest in political theory. The theoretical demand for a critique of the existent in the name of some nebulous better state of things is decried as mere intellectual arrogance. In fact, there is no state of things truly better than the one we have already achieved. This kind of objection can be heard today not only from the right but from the (former) left as well. Is something being said here beyond the disappointment with the promises of days gone by?

» «

Learning processes are dependent on better theories, not antitheoretical hostility. Besides, I can't agree with your description. In America, for example, we're experiencing a veritable boom in normative political theory. The protagonists are Rawls and Dworkin, Charles Taylor and Michael Walzer, Bruce Ackerman and Alistair MacIntyre. In England and here in Germany, 'civil society' is the subject of heated debates. I really don't see any exhaustion of theory.

» «

Then perhaps it's also a mood of resignation, one justified by the view that the political and social transformation of Europe is of secondary importance measured against the problems that we face as a result of the progressive destruction of the environment. Key terms: deforestation, air and water pollution, greenhouse effect. This rather apocalyptic mood can be felt from many politically exhausted young people. What do you make of it?

» «

You're talking about seismographic moods. It's true that the time bombs of a recklessly exploited natural world are ticking faintly and persistently. But it's also true that while nature, in its own way, plots its revenge for the mutilations we have inflicted on it, nature *also* lifts its voice in *us*. Adorno spoke evocatively of the 'mindfulness of nature in us.' The paralyzing sadness that overcomes us when confronted with a landscape destroyed, poisoned, literally asphyxiated by human hands and by the trash of civilization, is unmistakable. But on the other hand, the voice of our feelings would lose its own warning force if we melancholically give ourselves over to this sadness, or if the warning is suppressed by the urgency of our most immediate needs. We won't escape from the double bind of ecology and the market economy by getting sucked into the pull of these intuitive end-of-the-world moods. Instead, we have to let ourselves *learn* from our own feelings. Only further enlightenment – *docta spes* – has grown from the devastation of enlightenment. Totalizing critiques of reason – which reason itself brings to confusion – are worthless. *Nemo contra Deum nisi Deus ipse* – which is not to appeal to some sort of deified reason, but on the contrary to say that it is only through reason that we can determine the limits of our own rationality. *This* is the fundamental figure of Kantian thought that was definitive for modernity. And modernity can't just be peeled off like a dirty shirt. It's in our skin. We find ourselves in the condition of modern life: we didn't freely choose it; it is existentially unavoidable. But for the opened eyes of modernity, this condition also implies a challenge, and not just disaster.

»«

But isn't that a little unrealistic? The political and social changes in Europe that we've been talking about are becoming increasingly meaningless when compared to the rise of the kind of problems we discussed in connection with the Gulf War in the first part of this interview. Key terms: rising poverty and national debt in many Third World nations, increasing destitution in Africa and Asia – despite of or because of our so-called developmental aid. Many intellectuals in the Third World regard our form of political discourse as a grotesque Eurocentrism.

» «

No, Eurocentrism – expanded to include the North Atlantic – has a moment of objectivity. As its successors we see rather clearly the scale of destruction that the violent, global spread of industrial culture has inflicted, and continues to inflict, on even the most far-flung traditional cultures. The anonymous operation of world markets and television has taken over the task that was once handled by colonial masters and missionaries – even if things don't go so far as the barbarity of a high-tech military campaign. Imperialist domination has grown anonymous: it has 'sublated' itself into the domination of systemic imperatives – as well as the clandestine curriculum of a way of life that is registered in the material infrastructure of the world metropolises of the twenty-first century, exploding all the old European mentalities – in São Paolo and Cairo no differently than in Tokyo. But this progressive anonymity also shows the emergence of a new kind of vicious circle – that alien and familiar needs have entered into an uncanny and unholy union. It is this combination that has rendered the material world culture that first took shape in Europe into a mutely alternativeless force, at least for the time being. Looking at this fact doesn't mean *approving* of it. Indeed, the question isn't whether *this* is what we could have wanted. That would be an abstract question in the Hegelian sense. The question is whether Europe will use the second chance that it now has for the civilizing of the earth, for breaking out of the desperate circulatory process of imperialistic power politics.

I don't mean that this alternativeless material world culture should now embark on a second missionary expedition, in the sense of a project of spiritual subjugation. Occidental rationalism must go back into itself and overcome its own blindnesses in order to open up dialogically what it can learn from the traditions of other cultures. An intercultural encounter worthy of the name would also demand that the submerged elements of our own tradition be brought to light. Europe must use one of its strengths, namely its potential for self-criticism, its power of self-transformation, in order to relativize itself far more radically vis-à-vis the others, the strangers, the misunderstood. That's the opposite of Eurocentrism. But *we* can overcome Eurocentrism only out of the better spirit of Europe. Only if we are able to do this will the wounds inflicted on the world by Eurocentrism, and the material world culture that grew from it, become if not healed, then at least treatable.

These are somewhat too grand turns of phrase for characterizing the completely profane, piecemeal kind of perspectives that we need to work from. I've got a tin ear for Heideggerian melodies. 'Only a god can save us' – that's the kind of noble tone in philosophy that already got on Kant's nerves. Philosophers don't change the world. What we need is to practice a little more solidarity: without that, intelligent action will remain permanently foundationless and inconsequential. Such practice, certainly, requires rational institutions; it needs rules and communicative forms that don't morally overtax the citizens, but rather exact the virtue of an orientation toward the common good in small change.

If there is any small remnant of utopia that I've preserved, then it is surely the idea that democracy – and the public struggle for its best form – is capable of hacking through the Gordian knots of otherwise insoluble problems. I'm not saying that we're going to succeed in this; we don't even know whether success is possible. But because we don't know, we at least have to try. Apocalyptic moods sap the energies that nourish these initiatives. Optimism and pessimism aren't really relevant categories here.

What Theories Can Accomplish – and What They Can't

MICHAEL HALLER: *Herr Habermas, our reflections on social theory are intended as a way of bringing the contemporary experiences that you've mentioned into a broader context, of exploring their conditions and validity, and investigating the developmental history of our own society.*

Today we observe a certain weariness with theory itself; a kind of theoretical exhaustion intoned with resignation, particularly by sensitive people. Could this weariness be linked with a loss of historicity? And if so, could such a defensive reaction be based on anxiety for the future?

Let me take this even one step further: could this weariness with theory trace itself back to the simple fact that people are looking for a way out of panicked anxiety in the face of industrial society's impending annihilation of the very natural foundations of human existence?

» «

JÜRGEN HABERMAS: That's a lot of questions at once. The first key term was the 'weariness with theory' of young people. I don't quite know how you've arrived at this diagnosis. For years my books have sold evenly, whether well or poorly. I enjoy my students; they are committed, reasonably well read, and eager for discussion. Of course, compared with sociology, much more expectations are brought into contemporary philosophy. Young people today expect something more from philosophy, and they're naturally disappointed when their studies don't teach them how to solve the problems of their own lives – in Frankfurt, at any rate,

nobody claims to be able to tell them. Like sociology, philosophy is only a science, and it follows the dynamic of its
own problems – so we flatter ourselves, at any rate. To get
anything out of theoretical work, you have to follow it for
its own sake. There's a kind of therapeutic frustration that
goes along with this. Despite all the stories you hear, I've
always thought it was nonsense to launch interrogations
of cognitive interests without really becoming involved in
the matter oneself. This certainly doesn't mean that one
shouldn't also inquire into the ways that a theory is rooted
in life. An example of this would be the question of whether
the rise and fall of fashion in the human and social sciences
might not have something to do with pretheoretical experiences and historical contexts. Perhaps structuralist or
system-theoretical approaches, which banish subjects and
subjectivity from their basic concepts, make sense to the
anxious members of a society of risk only because, *before* all
science, they are simply overwhelmed by social complexity,
which they then encounter as a second nature. You see, I've
turned your question around somewhat. It isn't the denial
of theory as such, but rather the *appeal,* that grants a particular reception to a given theory at a particular moment,
that is related to the mood of the times – such as, for example, the relation between an interest in so-called chaos theory and the 'panicked anxiety' that you speak of.

In any case, it's good not to expect any more or anything
different from theories than what they can achieve – and
that's little enough.

»«

Your own social theory raises some very considerable claims.
It reflects prevailing social conditions in the light of an ideal
social formation, one in which persons operate as subjects who

through their actions aim at an intersubjective realization of the rational. This perspective allows you a critical illumination of existing conditions – conditions in which you, as a theorist, are also bound up. This calls to mind the comparison you once made with the psychoanalyst who, engaged in a therapeutic conversation with his patient, orients himself according to the ideal of a successful communicative relationship.

» «

In *Knowledge and Human Interests* I compared psychoanalysis with social theory. Of course, I was thinking of methodological structures and basic concepts. One must never imagine the addressees of social theory, or even society itself, as a subject writ large, whose eyes are to be opened by the social theorist. In a process of enlightenment, there are only participants. In any event, back then (for example, in the introduction to the new edition of *Theory and Practice*) I acted very quickly to dispel these sorts of misunderstandings – which I was perhaps not careful enough in avoiding. That's all over and done with.

Now, as far as the 'ideal society' goes, in whose light I am supposed to criticize the existent – there too things are a bit different. As opposed to my famous American colleagues such as Rawls and Nozick, I've never had any ambition of sketching out a normative political theory. Although it's perfectly sensible, I don't design the basic norms of a 'well-ordered' society on the drafting table. It's more a matter of the reconstruction of actual conditions, under the premise that in everyday communicative practice, sociated individuals cannot avoid *also* employing everyday speech in a way that is oriented toward reaching understanding. For this, they have to proceed from particular pragmatic presuppositions, in which something like communicative reason emerges. It's really quite simple: whenever we mean what we say, we raise the claim that what is said is true, or right, or truthful. With this claim, a small bit of ideality breaks into our everyday lives, because such validity claims can in the end be resolved only with arguments. At the same time, we know that arguments that appear valid to us today can prove to be false tomorrow, in light of new experiences and new information.

Everyday praxis oriented toward understanding is permeated with unavoidable idealizations. These simply inhere in the medium of the everyday language in which the reproduction of our lives takes place. Of course, as individuals we can at any time decide to manipulate others, or to act in an openly strategic manner. But in fact not everyone could behave in this way at any time. Otherwise, for example, the category of lying would become meaningless; the grammatics of our language would in the end have to collapse. Things like the appropriation of tradition or socialization would become impossible. In that case, we would be obliged to construct *other* concepts from social life and the social world than the ones we used to operate with, if we participate in such a life, and find ourselves in such a world. My point is that my references to idealizations have nothing to do with ideals that the solitary theorist sets up *in opposition to* reality; I am referring only to the normative contents that are *encountered* in practice, which we cannot do without, since language, together with the idealizations it demands of speakers, is simply constitutive for socio-cultural forms of life.

» «

In your work, you have called the definitive model followed by industrial society over the past two hundred years 'emancipa-

tion': humanity wishes to make decisions concerning its own good with increasing self-determination, that is, free from alien interests. As I understand you, this process of emancipation traces back to the idea that persons want to reach understanding with one another, that is, to restrain their own egoism and help the better argument to gain validity. But is this anything more than a beautiful ideal?

» «

In 1967, when Rias called on Adorno to speak on the subject of 'aesthetic models of the present,' Adorno responded that the popular concept of models was itself the problem. 'Model' still suggests the sort of substantive, general, binding orientations that are lost to us in modernity. They have been replaced by formalisms, by the procedural rationality of modes of action, that tell one only how one should go about doing something if one is aiming for a good outcome.

Since the end of the eighteenth century, when Kant spoke of the 'deliverance of humanity from its self-imposed immaturity,' concepts like 'enlightenment' and 'emancipation' have referred to processes in which one experiences in one's own person the self-transformations that occur when one learns to act rationally, according to formalized points of view. Enlightenment is a reflex of self-experience in the course of learning processes. Emancipation means something like the liberation from a confinement into which we imagine we have fallen, but for which we ourselves bear the responsibility, since it results neither from natural causality nor from the limitations of our own understanding. Emancipation is a very special kind of self-experience, because in it processes of self-understanding link up with an increase in autonomy. In this way, 'ethical' and 'moral' insights connect up with one another. If with 'ethical' questions we want to get clear on who we are and who we want to be, and if with 'moral' questions we want to know what is equally good for all, then moral insights are linked with a new ethical understanding in emancipatory consciousness. We learn who we are by simultaneously learning to see differently in relationships with others. Rejuvenations of this kind often trace back to adolescence, which is certainly a time of life in which we often productively work through painful crises in this way. The expression 'emancipation' thus has its place in the realm of the subject's relation with itself: it refers to discontinuous transformations in the practical self-relations of persons.

But if we want to translate this expression back into the social, where it originally came from (as a juridical term, 'emancipation' describes the setting free of slaves or the coming of age of children), we have to be careful not to force a conceptualism derived from the philosophy of the subject onto social conditions that it doesn't fit. Neither social collectives nor society as a whole can be regarded as a subject writ large. For this reason, I'm rather careful these days about using the expression 'emancipation' beyond the realm of biographical experiences. Rather, concepts like 'reaching understanding' and 'communicative action' have moved to the center of my thinking. They have a more trivial significance; that is, they refer to what goes on constantly in everyday practice – without the poetic or false-romanticizing luster of being somehow *extraordinary* experiences. Initially, this has nothing to do with morality either. We'll leave aside the fact that moral action cannot be explained by the contradiction between egoism and altruism, as you say it can – in fact, that which commands our feelings of duty often coincides with our own interests, even our immediate interests.

And yet I sense the traces of a concealed idealism in your Theory of Communicative Action, *an idealism that overlooks the forces that dominate political action – for example, strategic intentions. The annexation of the* GDR, *as it was railroaded through in 1990, is a perfect example of the manipulative power even of democratically legitimated politics. To exaggerate a bit, one could write a plausible history of the twentieth century as the continuing failure of rational argumentation.*

»«

First of all, we need to be able to explain why it is that we regard the revolution in the GDR – and in the whole of Eastern Europe – as a welcome process. This can hardly be described with the Kantian model of enlightenment any longer. Nevertheless, democratic institutions under the rule of law have established themselves against all the repression of a ghostly surveillance state. This new political constitution introduces rationally justifiable principles of right and justice – that is, principles that in a practical discourse could find a considered approval by all those affected by them.

Now, as far as the actual course of the unification process is concerned, we have to state in all seriousness that it proceeded, *grosso modo,* in harmony with the norms of our political order. Opening up legitimate spaces for strategic action is just what such a legally formed political order is supposed to do. The politics of the chancellor's office – the subject of our political argument – were naturally legal; they stayed within the space that was constitutionally conceded by the government. When party politics started to get out of hand and virtually all the parties began treating voting rights as nothing more than a maneuverable mass for their own speculations, the federal constitutional courts put a stop to the business.[1] That's the constitutionally legitimate side of the process. International treaties received parliamentary ratification, even if only as a packet. Democratic elections took place, and so forth. It's true that I've complained about the normative deficits from a political and a constitutional point of view. But this criticism didn't come from thin air. It doesn't appeal to principles that I just made up, but to principles that were achieved only over the course of centuries of struggles, and of the collective experience of social recognition that in the end were finally assimilated into our political culture. This is where we can actually talk about a history of political emancipation.

» «

What sorts of trends and processes would you mention if you wanted to indicate this history of emancipation in our own time?

» «

I think of the measure of individual freedom, social security, and political participation that has resulted in a higher value of, and greater consideration for, the lives of individuals in the more fortunate parts of our planet. Before the French Revolution, before the workers' movements in Europe, before the spread of formal secondary education, before the feminist movement, before the domestication of relationships of violence internal to families, prisons, hospitals, and so on, the life of an individual woman or man had less worth – not regarded from our own point of view, of course, but from the contemporary perspective. That's naturally only one side of the coin. Horkheimer and Adorno spoke of a 'dialectic of enlightenment.' This throws a certain light on the other side of the coin, on the horror of

the flip side of the mirror of enlightenment. But these criticisms and self-criticisms still sustain themselves from the
light of enlightenment – we have no other criteria, save for
its own. If they are to *remain* convincing, basic moral concepts such as autonomy and human dignity, solidarity, or
equality must also be able to transform themselves in the
course of processes of their own self-application, that is, in
the critical application of their own usage. Emancipation –
if we are to give this word a meaning that is foolproof
against all misunderstanding – makes humanity more independent, but not automatically happier.

Of course we don't have the ability to choose between a
more or a less conscious mode of living, since possibilities
for choice arise only with the act of coming to consciousness. On the other hand, criteria for happiness, for the
clinical evaluation of a more or a less unalienated, un-
deformed life are a rather precarious matter. Whoever still
believes in *these* criteria (which are hardly a matter of social
theory) will not, I suspect, come to the conclusion that
modern forms of life are in this clinical sense any better
than others. The concept of modernity no longer comes
with a promise of happiness. But despite all the talk of post-
modernity, there are no visible rational alternatives to this
form of life. What else is left for us, then, but at least to
search out practical improvements *within* this form of life?

» «

*If you take the recent historical experiences that we've been
discussing as a background, it's plausible to understand the
form of parliamentarianism that grew out of bourgeois society
as an institutionalization of a discourse that serves as a social
self-steering mechanism. Are democratic societies more rational – in the sense of rationality in the* Theory of Commu-

nicative Action – *than those societies that are organized on feudal, totalitarian, or other patterns?*

» «

There is a higher rationality in the sense of levels of learning potential. But we learn both in the cognitive dimension – think of the development of the forces of production – or in the moral and practical dimension – think of our post-metaphysically grounded moral and legal attitudes. We may well have even forfeited some sensibilities in other dimensions . . .

» «

Yes, but both the history and the functional analysis of parliamentarianism show that its function is the balancing of differing interests far more than the direction of discourse. The political platforms in Bonn or Washington follow (at best) the rules of the game of conflict resolution and compromise building. It's rare for anyone to demand the better argument.

» «

In systems of our type, compromise building goes a long way toward determining the political decision-making process. Who would argue with that? But these compromises are also rational, in the sense of a moral and practical procedural rationality, only if they are made according to the rules of a fair balancing of interests. And in turn, whether the rules themselves are fair, whether negotiations are properly institutionalized in relation to given power structures and interests, can only be decided in a discourse about questions of justice. But I don't want this reference to discourse to blur the important distinction between discourses in which the force of the better argument is what counts, on the one hand, versus compromises that the parties can agree to on *differing* grounds on the other. Whether it takes place in informal public communication or whether it is institutionalized in decision-making corporate bodies, the process of political will-formation doesn't *exhaust* itself in the aggregation and coordination of competing interest groups. Compromise makes up only one dimension of this process.

Today, all the information, presuppositions, programmatic ideas, indeed all the empirical and pragmatic factors that make up the basis for political decisions are controversial, because such interpretations are themselves by no means value-neutral. But how do you shake up the interpretations of existing states of affairs – prepared for the most part by experts – except with a critique that operates with better grounds? Even apart from this, there is no shortage of significant political issues that in fact touch on questions of justice. They're mostly cloaked as juridical deliberations, but they're also occasionally directly discussed as what they are: as moral and practical questions. In the unification treaty, a wealth of such questions had to be resolved; because the treaty was also a matter of complicated issues of distributive justice – for example, the controversial basic principle 'return before compensation'[2] – it was perceived as very problematic that all this was simply settled by the men with briefcases. Other issues, in turn, touch on questions of ethical and political self-understanding, questions of forms of life that we regard as desirable, or at least as bearable. Many ecological issues belong in this category. Minority conflicts, questions of the right of asylum, of the demands of new technologies, and so forth, demand that we come to a clear understanding on very serious value decisions – for instance, concerning how we as citizens of the Federal Republic understand what kind of society we want to live in.

When you analyze these different pragmatic, moral, and ethical questions, and reflect on which communicative forms demand a rational process of opinion- and will-formation, you see that political discussions do not come ready-made *only* in the form of compromise building. They form a vital network of diverse forms of argumentation and negotiation. It's not a coincidence that the implications of discourse theory have been carried the furthest in juridical discourses. But juridical discourses carry over into political decision-making processes. As in the institutionalization of legal proceedings, a piece of 'existing reason' can be found in the established rules and practices of opinion- and will-formation, from the parliamentarian rules of procedure to the organizational sections of the Basic Law. One can then connect up with this critically. The discourse-theoretical approach allows a critical relationship with the self-understanding of familiar political cultures, existing institutions, and recognized legal systems, with the goal of fully tapping the potential for self-transformation stored up within them.

» «

'Communicative action' is the term you use to refer to rational speech oriented toward agreement. In your theory, this action counts as the fundamental form of social conduct, since this action – as I understand your theory – is always already accompanied by an interest in reaching understanding: people talk to one another because they actually want to come to an understanding. In your theory, people act per se as rational, that is, as subjects capable of and prepared for consensus. In reality, of course, it's rare that people act as rational subjects; normally, their speech is loaded with differing motives and intentions having an awful lot to do with the desire for domina-

tion and subjugation – in the political sense, with the acquisi-
tion of power and the realization of particular goals. Is it un-
fair of me to imagine that – according to your theory – in an
emancipated society, subjects would behave toward one an-
other no longer like people, but as utterly rationalized think-
ing machines?

»«

First of all, I never say that people *want* to act communicatively, but that they *have to*. When parents bring up
their children, when the living appropriate the transmitted
wisdom of preceding generations, when individuals and
groups cooperate, that is, when they work to get along with
one another without the costly recourse to violence, they
all have to act communicatively. There are elementary social functions that can only be satisfied by means of communicative action. Our intersubjectively shared, overlapping lifeworlds lay down a broad background consensus,
without which our everyday praxis simply couldn't take
place. The Hobbesian state of nature, in which each iso-
lated bourgeois subject is alienated from all others, and
each is as wolf to the other (although real wolves live in
packs) – *that's* the truly *artificial* construction.

Furthermore, we can't equate communicative action
with argumentation. Communicative action normally takes
place in a common language and in a linguistically developed, preinterpreted world, in shared cultural forms of life,
normative contexts, handed-down traditions, customs,
routines, and so forth – in lifeworlds that are porous to one
another, that permeate and intertwine with one another.
This communicative action is not the same thing as argumentation. Arguments are improbable: they are heavily pre-
suppositioned forms of communication, islands in the sea

of praxis. This is why the talk about 'utterly rationalized thinking machines' is so far off the mark. It's indeed one of the most recent evolutionary accomplishments that arguments of a particular kind (e.g., legal or scientific arguments, or discussions of art criticism) are *institutionalized*, that is, are capable of being socially expected from particular persons at particular times in particular places.

Moreover, the great civilizing accomplishment of modern jurisprudence consists in the consensual (i.e., with the presumptive agreement of all citizens) prescription of regions of strategic action, as in the goal of the acquisition of private property or political power. This is just as true for the private legal arrangements of market commerce as it is for the public legal regulation of the competition of political parties or the employment of political power. Legal norms can have a compelling force over the long term only if the procedure that creates them is recognized as legitimate. In this moment of recognition, a communicative action appears on the other side of the legal system, so to speak; on the side of democratic will-formation and political legislation. While the subjects of private law may follow their own personal interests, citizens are to orient themselves toward the common good, to reach an understanding of their collective interests. Your reservations result from your somewhat too concretistic understanding of basic aspects of the theory of communicative action.

The 'emancipated society' is an ideal construction that invites misunderstanding. I'd rather speak of the idea of the undisabled subject. In general, this idea can be derived from the analysis of the necessary conditions for reaching understanding – it describes something like the image of symmetric relations of the freely reciprocal recognition of communicatively interacting subjects. Of course, this idea can't be depicted as the totality of a reconciled form of life and cast into the future as a utopia. It contains nothing more, but nothing less, than the formal characterization of necessary conditions for nonanticipatible forms of an un-disabled life. Socialism too ought never to have been conceived of as the concrete whole of a determinate, future form of life – this was the greatest *philosophical* error of this tradition. I've always said that 'socialism' is useful only if it serves as the idea of the epitome of the necessary conditions for emancipated forms of life, about which the participants *themselves* would have to reach understanding.

» «

But I'd like to persist with the question of whether a theory that aims at emancipation in the broadest sense, and that comes equipped with validity claims as sweeping as yours, is still appropriate for the urgent problems of the survival of industrial society. How can such an abstract theory hope to deal concretely enough with the dangers that we discussed earlier, with the idea of the 'society of risk'?

» «

Let's not get carried away. All your questions are essentially taking aim at the implications of my theoretical work for a diagnosis of contemporary conditions and problems, and it gives rise to the impression that I'm offering a theory that's supposed to be able to solve all of life's problems. You know how far removed I am from *that*. In general, I don't correspond to the traditional image of the 'philosopher' who explains the world with one thesis. Until now, we two have been having a conversation about political matters – and a little about what I understand by 'communicative reason.' But my daily work looks entirely different. There it's a matter of separate, already 'disassembled' problems that have their place in very different contexts. I visit separate problems where they live, in the scientific discourses where I find them. Then I make a contribution to this or that issue, let's say in the theory of speech acts or in moral theory, or in legal philosophy, in sociological discussions about processes of social rationalization, in philosophical discussions of the concept of modernity, on postmetaphysical thinking, and so on.

I don't force everything into one theoretical frame, and I don't assimilate everything into the basic concepts of a holistic master theory. Naturally, I make my contributions from my perspective, but one has to talk about philosophical questions philosophically, sociological questions sociologically, political questions politically. One has to know which discourse one is operating in, what tools one is employing, at which level of generality one is speaking. The philosophical dimension of this is merely the attempt not to lose the connections in the move from one discourse to another; not to let the categories freeze up, to keep the theoretical language fluid; to know, for example, where concepts like 'autopoesis' or 'self-consciousness' or 'rationality' belong – and above all, where they don't.

Nor should we let intelligent interviewers lead us into having an opinion on everything: I haven't taken part in the research in the areas of social risk. The degree of contemporary relevance that the concept of risk has acquired in various research contexts is due predominantly to a sea change in the political public sphere – the dangers to the ecology, the dangers of nuclear technology, of genetic research, and so on, are on everyone's lips. On the other hand, one also responds to change that has really happened. The growing interdependencies of world events and the simultaneously broadened horizon of expectations set loose corresponding experiences of disappointment and contingency; they shift temporal perspectives, change the structure of time consciousness itself, and so forth.

» «

Doesn't the traditional philosophy of consciousness have it much easier, in that it can still rely on the convincing power of the postulate of the ethics of responsibility?

» «

The philosophy of consciousness from Descartes through Kant up to Husserl took as its point of departure the fundamental question of epistemology and set to work on the question of subjectivity, that is, the relation of the representing subject to its own representations of objects. This philosophy forms a fruitful tradition, one to which we are all still related. Where would any of us be without our Kant? The great critics of the philosophy of consciousness, Heidegger on the one side, Wittgenstein on the other, have now led the way to a linguistic and pragmatic turn that today flips over, so to speak, and in the form of contextualistic views leads to a second historicism. In general, a world-creating subject – even a subject that internally reproduces its external environment – is no longer the point of departure for the philosophy of language. Therefore, this philosophy has to ask itself whether its new paradigm of reaching understanding between communicatively socialized subjects who always already find themselves in linguistically developed and intersubjectively shared lifeworlds – whether this paradigm has even reattained the old problem level. How can one talk about the problem of self-consciousness – or the self-reference of recursively self-enclosed systems – according to the principles of the theory of intersubjectivity? That's an exciting discussion that you're alluding to.

But I wouldn't relate this discussion immediately with problems of the ethics of responsibility. Your interest, Herr Haller, is primarily in the question of how theories that have wrapped themselves up in their own problems, and that have retreated so far into the scientific system under the pull of the social division of labor – how such autistic undertakings are at all able to place themselves in relation to praxis and to develop a force for the direction of action. Indeed, colleagues such as Luhmann[3] maintain that modern societies have simply collapsed into their various subsystems, which only build surrounding environments for one another and no longer have recourse to a common language, thus merely observing one another without being able to communicate anymore. But if this were true, your question would become objectless, and I don't believe that. The system-theoretical skepticism overlooks the eminent capability and productivity of socially circulating everyday speech, which (apart from the only other anthropological monopoly, the human hand) is the only faculty that has grown adequate to extraordinarily complex tasks precisely because it remained nonspecialized, because it hasn't been forced to specialize. On the other side, we can't simply gloss over the increasingly complex mediations between theory and praxis with ethical appeals.

All social theories are highly abstract today. At best, they can make us more sensitive to the ambivalences of development: they can contribute to our ability to understand the coming uncertainties as so many calls for increased responsibility within a shrinking field of action. They can open our eyes to dilemmas that we can't avoid and for which we have to prepare ourselves.

We've already talked about the political consequences of *one* such dilemma. Bureaucratic socialism emerged in its time as the dialectical response to the structural blindness of the capitalist economic system. Marx believed that any civilization that totally subjected itself to the imperatives of the self-valuation of capital carried the seed of its own destruction within it, because it blinded itself to any relevant factors that couldn't be expressed in terms of price. This thesis isn't falsified simply because Marx was himself blind to the potential for self-transformation – particularly the capacities for democratic countersteering – that are built into the institutions of the legal state. Today, we stand before the – predictable – wreckage of an experiment that has walked a gruesome path, a path that was prolonged by Stalinist barbarism. But the victor – even if the learning processes of the social state have considerably altered his original point of departure – doesn't simply stand justified at the end of this path. In view of the problems of the twenty-first century, the old doubt that once set loose those false reactions returns in a new form – the doubt whether a civilization *as a whole* can allow itself to be pulled into the whirlpool of the driving forces of one of its subsystems, even if this subsystem has become the pacemaker of evolution: whether it can let itself be sucked into the undertow of a self-referentially sealed economic system whose self-stabilization requires the absorption and the processing of all relevant information solely in the business management language of cost effectiveness. Nevertheless, the evident victims of the monstrously failed alternative to this tempt us to smother this doubt, that a spur to production has to *remain* – and that's what I mean by the dilemma.

*In a society surrounded on all sides by doomsday scenarios –
or perhaps chimeras – many people are inclining toward regarding the practical use-value of a theory as its only criterion
of value – thus effectively circumventing the question concerning the relation between social theory and everyday praxis. In
this connection, a phrase of Adorno's occurs to me. 'I believe
that one can very well direct philosophical criticism toward
the concept of absolute reason,' he wrote in his essay 'Education toward Maturity,' 'but one won't be able to deny that, apart
from thought, that is, apart from an unwavering, insistent
thinking, something like the determination of the right thing to
do, correct praxis as such, is impossible.' To pose our final
question: is this a sentence that could also stand as a motto
over your own thought and work?*

» «

Persistent thinking is certainly not enough, but without it
you don't get very far. Philosophical thought – by which I
mean not just professional philosophy but the work of productive scientists of all kinds – is not completely absorbed
into the anonymity of the research process. At the end of
the twentieth century too, philosophical thought appears
withdrawn, cocooned in esotericism. But however great its
distance from the concrete appears to be, philosophical
thought nevertheless communicates with contemporary
experiences in more intimate ways than through the con-
tinuously progressive work of scientific research. Philosophical thought is the expression of a sensibility for not-
yet-destroyed phenomena. The eccentricities of Luhmann's
systems theory, for example, reflect a quite naïve, prescien-
tific experience of a stage of complexity where world history took a step in the direction of a global society, and thus
created entirely new kinds of interdependences – inter-

twinings that outstrip subjects, their interventions, and their intentions, and render earlier conceptions of social self-organization and self-steering obsolete. Derrida's subtle conception of difference (which not coincidentally finds its strongest echo in the United States) expresses another aspect of this same experience – the fantastic unbinding of cultures, forms of life, styles, and world perspectives that today no longer simply encounter each other, but mutually open up to one another, penetrate each other in the medium of mutual interpretation, mix with one another, enter into hybrid and creative relationships, and produce an overwhelming pluralism, a decentered, hence obscure multiplicity, indeed a chaos of linked but contingent, nearly undecipherable sounds and texts. In relation to this, Foucault's microanalysis of power calls our attention to an invisible dialectic between the egalitarian tendencies of the age and those new unfreedoms that settled into the pores of simultaneously emancipated and systematically distorted communicative practices. Not for nothing was he, Foucault, fascinated by his late encounter with the *Dialectic of Enlightenment,* as he told me himself. But Adorno's aesthetic thinking, a thinking that tirelessly orbits the constellation of the nonidentical, has something more to say to us. It is a thinking that stands as the indelible register of the experience of the emigrant, faced with the sheer accident of his own escape from the death camps. Like the others, I am a generation younger. As the shock of *those* images and reports reached me, I was sixteen years old. I knew that, despite everything, we would live on in the anxiety of regression, that we would have to carry on in that anxiety. Since then I cast about, sometimes here, sometimes there, for traces of a reason that unites without effacing separation, that binds without unnaming difference, that points out the common and the shared among strangers, without depriving the other of otherness.

Your quote, Herr Haller, shows that my intention also establishes a link with Adorno. If it's definable at all, the nonidentical would be defined precisely through the fragility, the very dis-able-ability of its integrity. It is a kind of covering term for that emphatic concept of the individual that previously had been preserved for us in religious language. But Adorno knew that 'nothing of theological content continues in its existence untransformed; each moment of theological content must put itself to the test, to immigrate into the secular and the profane.'

The Asylum Debate (Paris Lecture, 14 January 1993)

I would like to begin by describing the circumstances and immediate context in which an issue as dry as asylum rights could have become the object of such heated controversy.[1] I will then go on to discuss the content and characteristics of this disingenuous debate in order finally to deal with the historical background of a peculiarly German conception of nationhood and citizenship, as well as the current question of whether this German mentality is regenerating itself in the wake of national unification.

«1» The circumstances of this unhappy debate include, first, the movements of global migration that are streaming into the peaceful and prosperous countries of Europe and North America from all the regions of the world afflicted with civil war and poverty. There are explosive imbalances between the economically developed societies of the North, on the one side, and the former colonies of the South and the states that, having emerged as a consequence of the collapse of the Soviet Union in the East, have long been excluded from the world market. These asymmetrical relationships can no longer (or at least not primarily) be characterized as relations of exploitation, since neither side can survive without the resources of the other. In classic situations of exploitation, the oppressed classes at least possess a veto power; for example, they can employ the threat of strikes insofar as their labor power is indispensable. Leaving aside the arsenals of weapons still stored in their territories, the South and the East no longer have access to corresponding sanctions. Whatever kinds of sanctions that remain accessible to these countries, and that could have real repercussions on the asymmetries, are rather masochistic ones: they could certainly 'threaten' with nuclear blackmail, with the global consequences of the depletion of their environmental resources, or even with a deluge of immigrants. The migration problem can be solved only if competitive economic systems can be developed in these regions as well – and the prospects for this are not good. Max Weber was right: capitalism developed within such a determinate sociocultural framework that this model cannot be transported to other cultures and other traditions without long-term processes of adaptation, if indeed it can be transplanted at all. This is something we can observe even in our own countries, for example south of Rome. The causes of the problem of global migration are just as difficult to manage as are its consequences for those countries that have been hardest hit by immigration. That there are no simple solutions is the premise for all my further reflections.

Countries such as Germany and France, which in contrast to the United States are not nations of immigrants in the classic sense, have been the most affected by the torrent of immigration. Historically, Germany is a nation of emigrants. Now it is being painfully transformed into a nation of immigrants. Of course, both Germany and France recruited an immigrant labor force out of their own self-interest in the 1960s and the early 1970s – at least until 1973–74. Provoked in part by the oil crisis, the German and French governments then adopted rather restrictive measures demanding a policy of repatriation. Today, the so-called guest workers – mainly from the South in France, and from Turkey and Yugoslavia in Germany – make up a considerable portion of the working population. They are overrepresented in the low-paying branches of the economy avoided by the indigenous population and have an above-average rate of unemployment. Meanwhile, families have followed; a second and a third generation have been born here. In short, fellow countrymen and -women are created from out of the ranks of immigrants. In order to avoid conflict, these people must now become citizens – in the legal as well as in the political-cultural sense of citizenship.

In the Federal Republic today, the problem of integrating the stream of newly arrived immigrants, as well as those who are already established here, takes place within a particular context. Here I will mention only two facts: the economic and political consequences of national unification, and right-wing terror.

«a» From an economic point of view, German unification has produced the ironic result that the worldwide economic slump only became noticeable in Germany after a delay of two years. The policy of financing the accrued costs of unification by assuming new debt took the form of an enormous program of governmental economic speculation, and it had, at first, a positive effect on Germany's western states. Now, however, the export-dependent Federal Republic is caught in the same downward trend as the rest of the world. In the old Federal Republic, the number of unemployed has topped the two-million mark, reminding us of the costs of transferring billions of deutsche marks from West to East – an act whose consequences the population found it easy to overlook under the influence of phony prognoses and false promises. From a social-psychological

point of view as well, the administratively orchestrated unification has led to disappointments on both sides. The normative deficits of the unification process that the intellectuals had complained about from the very beginning consist above all in the fact that no public debate ever took
place concerning the self-understanding of an expanded
Federal Republic, constructed out of such heterogeneous
parts. There was no constitutional debate; the debate that
stood in for it, over Berlin as the new capital, was played out
on the wrong fronts. The distinctive mentalities that characterize East and West are colliding even more violently. A
spiral of mutually opposed stereotypes has been set in motion, making it even more difficult to overcome the economic and social disparities between the two parts of Germany.

«b» In this tense situation, the unexpected outbreak of
radical right-wing violence is explosive. The 1992 year-end
balance sheet of the Hamburg-based Bureau for the Protection of the Constitution (published in the *Frankfurter Allgemeine Zeitung* on 19 December 1992) is shocking. During
1992, 17 people were murdered by right-wing radicals; between 800 and 900 were injured; in total, there were 2,200
attacks. According to the Bureau, the known right-wing
extremists are unevenly divided between the old and the
new Federal Republic: 2,600 in the old western states compared with 6,500 in the new eastern states, although the
latter make up only one-fifth of the total population. It is
certainly true that the organizational level of the groups in
the former GDR is rather low, while in the West the political
parties to the right of the CDU have had quite a large clien-
tele in state parliamentary elections ever since 1988. In the
last regional elections in Berlin and Bremen, 18 percent of

young male voters cast their ballots for right-wing parties. As in all of Europe, of course, these changing voting patterns also express a general level of resentment against the established political parties, which are themselves being objectively overwhelmed by the nature and the scope of the problems that await solutions today. This rejection of the established political parties is a disturbing symptom of a dwindling acceptance of political pluralism. What is shocking about this changed mentality (which in any event had been waiting in the wings for several years but has only in the last few months begun to manifest itself in the public sphere) is not so much the youth gangs who are pressing the old Nazi symbols back into service for the first time, but rather the fact that this political criminality, taken up in the media, has succeeded in awakening a familiar syndrome of prejudices in the broader population. The hatred of foreigners has frequently been translated into anti-Semitism as well as resentment against the disabled and other minority groups. This is the background for the sharp criticisms leveled against leftist intellectuals such as Günter Grass and the grotesque efforts of neoconservatives to trace right-wing terrorism back to the liberal changes in values and attitudes that appeared to have taken place in the Federal Republic over the course of the last two decades.

«2» In this context, the ruling coalition parties have given in to the temptation to fight out the issue of the so-called abuse of asylum rights from opportunistic points of view, so that on the one hand they could keep the more agitated portion of their voter bases from drifting over to the right-wing parties, while on the other hand they could characterize the opposition as the truly guilty party. Rather than stand up to this pressure, the timid leadership of the

SPD allowed the Petersburg Turn to bring the conflict into its own ranks.[2] This course of adaptation resulted in the dubious asylum compromise in the beginning of December 1992 – a compromise with which the parties tried once again to put an issue that had become far too hot for them on the political back burner.

For a long time, the CSU has operated according to the principle that, if it works for Schönhuber, do what Schönhuber is doing.[3] Ever since the attacks in Rostock, the asylum debate has signaled clearly that this maxim has found supporters far beyond the Bavarian border, indeed deep into the rank and file of the SPD. While still general secretary of the CDU, Volker Rühe prodded his party into putting the asylum question on the political agenda. When the sympathizing population of Rostock set up sausage stands in front of the burning asylum shelters, the message went out loud and clear that the task facing the majority-tenders was to be no offensive project of conviction, but rather symbolic politics – a politics of constitutional alterations that cost nothing and change nothing, but that do succeed in getting the point across to even the dimmest of wits: the problem with the hatred of foreigners is the foreigners themselves. In September 1991, forty-eight hours after the first dramatic outbreak of antiforeigner violence in Hoyerswerda, the Israeli ambassador contacted the foreign ministry because he had heard no announcement of a clear position by the federal government. But after Rostock, too, the government gave no hint of moral outrage, sympathy, or democratic wrath against the return of attitudes and affects that can only lead to the destruction of a political community. The chancellor's fury was limited to the handful of hecklers at the Berlin super-demonstration, insofar as they damaged Germany's appearance in the eyes of the rest of the world: for him, this was the real crime. Even after Mölln,[4] all that occurred to the editors at the *Frankfurter Allgemeine Zeitung* (24 November 1992) was 'the love for one's own country, which one must not expose to disgrace.'

It is in fact these reactions to the right-wing terror – reactions from the political center of the population and from the government, the state apparatus, and the leadership of the political parties – that constitute the phenomenon of a second 'German Autumn.'[5] The most pressing concern was neither the victims nor the de-civilizing of our society, but rather the reputation and esteem of Germany as an industrial leader. Even after the murders in Mölln – murders that provoked widespread outrage and spontaneous sympathy with the Turkish victims – an administration spokesman explained the absence of the chancellor by referring to business more pressing than 'condolence tourism.' The problem wasn't the skinheads – it was the police, who either weren't around or who looked on without intervening; it was the prosecuting authorities who dragged their feet, until they were dealing with Jewish counterdemonstrators from France; it was the courts, who handed out incomprehensible sentences; it was army officers who threw their practice hand grenades at asylum shelters; it was political parties that diverted attention from the real problems of a badly engineered unification process with their asylum debate, and who succeeded in turning a dull, resentment-laden portion of the electorate into their accomplices. I can recall no other issue that has been so zealously dragged out and kept alive in the public media and yet, at the same time, has been made so obscure and unrecognizable. Behind the smoke screen of this deceitful asylum debate, the old Federal Republic has changed more profoundly and more rapidly in the last quarter of 1992 than it had in the preceding fifteen years.

Let me briefly introduce four aspects of this obscured and obscuring debate.

«a» The insincerity in the public treatment of the asylum question begins with *false definitions*. The talk of 'misuse' of the right to asylum conceals the fact that we need an immigration policy that opens other legal options for immigrants. Questions of political asylum and immigration form a single package. For example, despite the large number of illegal immigrants in the United States, the official annual quota for immigration was raised to 714,000. With us in Germany, no one dares even lead the discussion toward questions of the size and specific composition of the quota of immigrants, which (as the churches rightly insist) cannot be limited to 'desirable skilled workers.' Those who do touch on the taboo are more comfortable talking about 'immigration limits.' The inherent defect of the asylum-rights compromise struck by the administration and the SPD in the beginning of December 1992 lies in the fact that the preamble promises an immigration policy – and a transformed naturalization policy – that the text of the compromise itself never delivers. Now, as in the past, the guidelines for naturalization rights make it clear that we are not a nation of immigrants, and we don't want to become one.

«b» The dishonesty continues in the *politics of information*. Relevant data were distributed incompletely or with long delays and were misleadingly interpreted. As opposed to the 440,000 people who claimed asylum last year, 220,000 immigrants entered the country who, according to a dubious interpretation of Article 116 of the Basic Law, are of

'German descent' and therefore possess a claim to German citizenship. As early as 1990, Oscar Lafontaine raised the question of whether the designation of these so-called 'status Germans' is at all compatible with the basic principles of a liberal constitution. But the argument that German citizens constitute a legal community [*Rechtsgemeinshaft*] and not an ethnic community [*Volksgemeinschaft*] seems to have had no effect. The largest contingent of asylum seekers by far comes from Yugoslavia; numbering approximately 130,000, these immigrants are now finally supposed to be designated as war refugees, separated out of the asylum process, and granted a temporary right to remain. It is a little-known fact that asylum seekers who are already established and living in Germany – a category that comprises roughly one-third of the total number of applications for asylum – may no longer be deported on the basis of international law. This fact changes the picture for a quota of accepted asylum applications of only 5 percent. These three examples are meant to show there is still no realistic breakdown of the global figures on immigration. And we also have to factor in the number of immigrants that the shrinking population of the Federal Republic needs out of its own self-interest, if it is to keep the social security system from collapsing under the weight of a top-heavy age pyramid. The contributions to the national economy that foreign workers have made and continue to make remain unmentioned, as has the statistically undocumented internal emigration from eastern to western Germany, which continues to put a considerable strain on the intake capacity of the old Federal Republic.

«c» What pushes the asylum debate the furthest into the gray area between deception and self-deception is the suggestion that a change in the Basic Law could solve the problem. In fact, far more (indeed virtually everything that could effectively be done) can happen immediately within the existing laws, or at any rate without a change in the Basic Law. The acceptance process could be simplified to involve only one authority, and the time needed to handle individual cases could be reduced to four months. For this to happen, of course, the 4,000 positions planned for the responsible government bureau would actually have to be staffed; at present 2,500 of them remain unfilled. However, the government's loud demands for the elimination of individual asylum rights (Articles 16 and 19 of the Basic Law) are already ruled out on constitutional grounds. This is the position not only of the federal constitutional justice Kühling, the federal administrative judge Rothkegel, and the former Hessian Data Protection Officer Spiros Simitis; looking back at the connection between political asylum and the measure of human dignity guaranteed by Article 1, it is also supported by all previous jurisdictions of the Federal Constitutional Court. Until there is a more comprehensive European harmonization of asylum and immigration laws, an expansion of the Basic Law is at issue only for those asylum seekers who have submitted an application in countries where the Geneva convention on refugees and the European convention on human rights are in force, and who have already been turned down by those countries. The sheer fact of entry from so-called 'secure third states' is in no way sufficient for turning away asylum seekers at the border (as the asylum compromise calls for). Talk of asylum rights as a right of mercy [*Gnadenrecht*] or as institutional guarantee, like the talk of appeals committees and tribunals, was nothing but con artistry. In any case, these options wouldn't be of much help. If Herr Seiters[6] had the United States' experiences with illegal immigrants from Mexico before him, he'd see the futility of his fantasies of circling the wagons. He couldn't control the tide of immigration even if – as is now being planned – he were allowed to fortify the eastern border with an electronic Maginot Line.

«d» Of course, the flaw of the recently concluded asylum compromise consists not only in its attempt to shift the burden of asylum seekers traveling overland from eastern Europe onto our neighbors – Poland, the Czech Republic, and Austria. Nor does it consist only in the introduction of problematic lists of 'persecution-free' countries. (The most recent reflections of our foreign minister show where this particular plan is heading: the suggestions that he offered in London were designed to lend credence to the supposition that refugees from Bulgaria, Ghana, Liberia, Nigeria, Pakistan, Romania, Togo, Zaire, and Turkey are not politically persecuted.) Above all, the asylum compromise commits the error of leaving things precisely as they were with respect to naturalization rights, instead of making the application process for citizenship easier for foreigners who are already established in Germany. As opposed to France, which employs the principle of territory, Germany determines nationality according to the principle of descent. This leads to the result, for example, that up until reunification, not just the citizens of the Federal Republic but also all the citizens of the GDR were German nationals. Now as in the past, the so-called *Volksdeutschen* – above all, Poles and Russians – who can prove a German ethnicity have a claim to German citizenship. In contrast, resident guest workers in Germany are denied dual citizenship. Nor do their children who have been born in Germany automatically receive the right to citizenship, as is usual in France. While immigrants in France can apply for citizenship after five years, this is only possible in Germany after fifteen years, even for those willing to renounce their prior citizenship.

«3» These differences in naturalization policies are expressions of a distinct national self-consciousness – one that forms the historical background against which the asylum debate has to be judged. In a recent study, (*Citizenship and Nationhood in France and Germany*, Cambridge, Mass., 1992), the American historian Rogers Brubaker has set up an instructive comparison between the politically centralized, more or less assimilationist self-understanding of the French as a nation of citizens, on the one side, and on the other side the culturally and linguistically centered, ethnically differentiated self-understanding of the Germans as a nation of *Volksgenossen*. Whoever lives in France and possesses the rights of a French citizen counts as French, while with us, subtle distinctions were still being made right up until the end of the last war between '*Deutschen*,' that is, German citizens of German descent, '*Reichsdeutschen*,' or German citizens of non-German (for example Polish) descent, and '*Volksdeutschen*,' or those of German descent with non-German citizenship.

In France, national identity was able to develop within the framework of an existing geographically defined state; in Germany, national identity had to link itself up with the educated middle classes' romantically inspired vision of a cultural nation. This conception set up an imaginary unity, one that was obliged to support itself in the commonalities of language, tradition, and ethnicity in order to move beyond the realities of the small states that actually existed and the troubled alternatives of small-German versus great-German solutions. Still more influential was the fact that French national consciousness could develop simultaneously with the achievement of democratic civil rights and from the struggle against the sovereignty of their own king, while German nationalism emerged from a struggle against Napoleon, that is, against an external foe, long before the development of a nation-state under Bismarck and completely independent of any achievement of democratic civil rights. Thus, nationalism in France remained deeply rooted in the mythology of the French Revolution and could always reassure itself of its connection with the universalistic ideas of popular sovereignty and human rights, while in Germany nationalism emerged from the context of a war of liberation, and thus remained ensnared in passionate notions of the uniqueness of culture and ethnicity. This particularism has molded our national self-understanding far more deeply.

An echo of this particularism could be heard in speeches delivered in Jena in January 1993. According to the *Frankfurter Rundschau*'s coverage of a meeting of the umbrella organization of the German student societies [*Burschenschaften*] (11 January 1993), 'The majority of the German student societies spoke out in favor of promoting "a concept of the fatherland based on national character" [*volkstumsbezogenen Vaterlandsbegriff*] as a political goal. According to the societies' own self-conceptions, the fatherland is not to be equated with national borders; over the long term, political developments in Europe will lead to a situation where national borders can alter themselves "from the inside, according to the will of each nation."'

After 1945 – that is, after the gradual process of dealing

with the shocking barbarism of the mass crimes of National Socialism – the old Federal Republic had turned its back on this sort of 'special consciousness.' Its position at the frontier of a world bilaterally divided between the two superpowers contributed to this process. The dissolution of the Soviet Union and German reunification have resulted in an essential transformation of this situation. For this reason, reactions to the reemergence of right-wing radicalism – and in this context, the emergence of the asylum debate as well – raise the question of whether the expanded Federal Republic is going to continue on the path toward political civilization, or whether it will reintroduce the old special consciousness in a new form. Of course there won't be any single, sweeping answer to this question. Instead, the answers must differ according to whether we are looking at the old or the new federal states.

There are obvious explanations for the return of the old stereotypes in the former GDR. Normally, painful processes of 'creative destruction' in which old capitals are devalued and new capacities are created take place over long periods of time and in particular locations. After the currency reform, this process hit the economy, and from there the population of the GDR, everywhere and all at once. The devaluation of industrial capital is symbolically embodied in the Trust Corporation [*Treuhandgesellschaft*] that squanders the nation's wealth; the devaluation of the personal-historical capital of entire generations is expressed in the anonymous fates of mass unemployment. The devaluation of intellectual capital emerges with the liquidation of colleges and universities, in the forced reconfiguration [*Gleichschaltung*] of the media – and not least in the zealously pursued task of discrediting once-influential intellectuals: the so-called 'literature controversy' has done its job. If one adds to all this the fact that the characteristic features of a rather 'German' mentality could keep better in a state-socialist container than they did in the West, then youth gangs demolishing cars and setting off street battles with baseball bats – even the right-wing radicals themselves – come as no surprise. In the *Spiegel* (11 January 1993) we read: 'Right after the *Wende*, a youth scene marked by anxiety, rage, and disorientation following the collapse of the GDR ran headlong into the old and the neo-Nazis from the West, [finding] common ground in the task of reestablishing an aggressive, authoritarian "Germanness."' We need to face the fact that the milieu that produces such a proclivity for violence can change only along with 'conditions,' and not overnight. It is different in the western part of the country, where the conditions have not changed, but where the flood-gates have opened.

Here in the West, there has been a change in the limit-values that have been built into the circulatory process of a democratic public sphere. Today the unspeakable – something that a fifth of the population may have thought, but up until now never expressed in public – is cresting over the banks. This phenomenon, a lowering of thresholds, can't be explained away by the failures of families and schools. It's not the young who are the problem, but rather the adults, not the core of violence but the shell in which it thrives. Naturally, a scene of insecure, disoriented, and disappointed young people has emerged in the West as well as the East – youths whose latent potential for violence can be touched off by the wrong signals (like ordering the police to pull back from burning asylum shelters) and can be exploited by right-wing ideologues. But this can gain a power of infection only within the milieu of a heartless prosperity chauvinism, one that can transform rampaging youths into 'projection figures of social fantasies of violence.' The conservative politicians' current efforts to ease the problem by reducing right-wing radicalism to an educational problem – as with their worn-out slogan 'courage for education' – is, for this reason, a fatal diversionary tactic. Instead, what they are doing is shrinking a clear boundary to the right. I am assuming that in the old federal states it's not so much the social situation that has changed as its perception.

Since all perceptions are interpreted, it's the interpretations that we must look at. What has changed since 1989? Not only have anxieties about the future grown but also the collective that people would like to look to for support, if not absorption. Hans Magnus Enzensberger believes that the Federal Republic is suffering from a 'Big Lie': the illusion that reunification was what we always wanted. Even if we limit this diagnosis to the old Federal Republic, it would hardly be correct for the majority of the population under fifty years old, who had to get used to the unexpected reunification – and the other Germany – only bit by bit. This couldn't have been otherwise, and they certainly have no need to kid themselves about it now.

Naturally Enzensberger knows the phenomenon he's talking about. Big Lies are pathologies that stabilize themselves through their own existential usefulness. During the Adenauer era, the Big Lie that we all had to deal with was one issued from on high: 'we're all democrats here.' The Federal Republic needed a very long time to get over this. It took a youth revolt to free the Federal Republic from the devastating socio-psychological effects of this self-deception. If there really is a second Big Lie that has emerged since 1989, it's far more the lie that 'we have finally become normal again.' A feeling of relief hides behind the ambiguous formula 'farewell to the old Federal Republic.' Beyond its trivially correct meaning, this farewell is loaded with peculiarly irrational overtones. The triumphant sigh of relief palpable in the statement that 'we are finally a normal nation-state again' asks that we take a perspective from which the still-celebrated 'history of success' of the Federal Republic now appears as the real 'special path': one that is supposed to have embodied the enforced abnormality of a defeated and divided nation. The clichés are on everyone's lips: we need to break out of our shell; we need no longer bend over backwards to be moral model pupils; we should stop shrinking from the hard realities; we should stop being so coy and should assume a leadership role in Europe, instead of reacting to the fate of the world with teary-eyed sensitivity.

Arnulf Baring has made himself the eloquent champion of this piquant reversal of the *Sonderweg* hypothesis. In a lecture given to the Martin Schleyer Foundation, he explores the new nexus of German interests. Germany after reunification is for Baring once again the old one. 'We still live, we live since 1990 once again in the Germany of Bismarck.' For Baring, Germany is no longer a purely Western European country: it lies once again in Central Europe. What falls into our laps in this manner is a global position for Germany 'that we tried, twice over, to seize violently in the first half of the century: Germany as the relative premier power of Europe. Before 1945 we attempted to force our will on Europe; very clumsily, I admit, and with catastrophic consequences as its result. Now we risk committing the opposite mistake in the face of the new challenges that our situation has presented us: refusing a greater share of responsibility.' For Baring, we now need to relearn how to perceive our own interests; how to make our demands plausible to our fellow European citizens; how to develop a healthy national consciousness; to 'win a deeper understanding of, and an alternate relationship to, our own history . . . [we must] go further back than 1945.' The normalcy of the German nation-state signifies here not only its expansion in social space but also the reconstitution of an unbroken continuum in time. In hindsight, the old Federal Republic now appears as the 'Adenauerian Federation of the Rhine' which, with its cosmopolitan, republican features, might, if need be, serve as a resource for the *Bismarckreich*. No longer acting 'clumsily,' as it did in the first two tries, the new Germany should now settle itself at the summit of a European league of nations with 20, 30, or 40 members, while nevertheless holding on at all costs to its own currency, since 'the deutsche mark is not merely a medium of payment but a symbol of our self-confidence as well.'

This multifaceted deutsche mark–nationalism, prepared with the finest historical acuity, reinstates the primacy of foreign policy and restores the lost honor of Treitschke's sense of *Realpolitik*. It already revealed itself in the desire for normalization visible among the advocates of a military intervention in the war in the Persian Gulf, and today it expresses itself in calls for a German seat on the UN Security Council and participation in international military operations, in opposition to the Maastricht Treaty and a Western-anchored European Union, and complaints over a Germany 'for which charity has sometimes seemed to begin in Europe, rather than at home' (*Frankfurter Allgemeine Zeitung*, 28 November 1992).

Of course, all these false accents aren't enough to lend any plausibility to the slogan that we've finally become a normal nation-state again – as if there even existed anything approaching the sort of nation-state that could answer the distant ideological echoes of the nineteenth century; as if the old-new Federal Republic, which is enmeshed in the global net of political and economic interdependencies more deeply than any other nation, could ever be propped up again with this antiquated model. There is no shortage of indications for what the mental farewell from the old Federal Republic might produce in the public consciousness of the new one.

At the higher levels, the 'call back to history' [*Rückruf in die Geschichte*][7] hasn't fallen on deaf ears. At the Wuppertal Playhouse, *Schlageter*-texts by the Nazi poet Hanns Johst are garnished with *Lieder* and poems by Heinrich Heine; at the Frankfurt Museum of Architecture the works of the (at that time no less known) architect Paul Schmidthenner are offered as a blueprint for the construction of a purely independent German path into modernism – straight past the Bauhaus. The boys at the *feuilleton*, meanwhile, have broken out of Frankfurt and swarmed clear across the country and are occupying themselves with the demolition of the literature of the old Federal Republic.[8] Armed with saber-rattling ideas from the old young-conservative attic, they're ready to put paid to the '68ers. At the middle levels, something even more crudely constructed is noticeable. The concerned editorialist at the *Frankfurt Allgemeine Zeitung*, looking into the shadow world of 'delegated democracy' where there were comrades who dared to contradict the Petersburg party leadership, observes a 'delirium of the ethics of conviction' and explains this undemocratic situation with the fairy-tale 'special path' hypothesis: 'In the shadow of the great global conflict, the culture of an everyday utopianism was able to flourish in West Germany, and in particular in West German social democracy, which had become the receptacle for a good portion of the political protest generation of 1968. Because the influence of German politics on the course of the world was extremely slight, one could assume global responsibility from one's own sheltered corner.' At the lowest levels, which the higher ones naturally dread, right-wing rock sends out the frank message: 'Our rights are in question / We'll get rid of this lousy plague. . . . / We have to fight for our race / German *Volk*, let's show them what we're made of.'

In the streets of Germany's big cities, of course, resistance has been stirring since November 1992. As Klaus Hartung has observed, it has been the leftist, liberal popular base that, ever since the (shamefully reinterpreted) mass demonstration in Berlin, has put an end to the half-hearted, ambiguous reactions from above. The most recent demonstrations show that the protest culture that developed over the course of the 1980s is now drawing from wider circles. A political rock festival in Frankfurt attracted over 200,000 young people. Munich and Berlin have been the sites of the largest demonstrations in the history of the Federal Republic. The initiative for the candlelight processions, in which between 200,000 and 400,000 people took part, didn't come from the political parties. It arose spontaneously from the midst of civil society. The murders of the Turkish woman and two Turkish girls in Mölln has released an unmistakable political effect: the people in the streets are defending the standards of a way of civil collective life that had been halfway taken for granted in the old Federal

Republic. The population is better than their politicians and spokespersons. Unless I'm fooling myself, this popular protest is continuous with those better traditions of the old Federal Republic – traditions that can only grow from the well-considered rejection of the kind of 'normalcy' that is now being invoked as an exemplar once again.

Behind the coffins of the victims of right-wing violence, republican consciousness appears to have reawakened. It is perhaps here that we can clearly see the alternatives to which the spokespersons and politicians, stuck in the old political order, remain oblivious. The political scene is truly taking on a new form: not because of the collapse of a left gazing proudly back at the contribution their 'alarmism' made to the development of the mentality of the old Federal Republic, but rather because of a schism among the liberal-conservatives. Now that the unifying bond of anti-communism has vanished, all those republicans who took their republicanism seriously as far back as the Adenauer period are splitting from the habitual republicans [*Gewohn-heitsrepublikaner*] who are setting off toward new shores. Now it's time for liberals to break away from all those who would wrap themselves in the threadbare, social-Darwinistic images of the collective self-assertion of a nation, rather than thinking in the colder and barer concepts that constitute the emancipatory protocols of a community under the rule of law.

Afterword (May 1993)

'Anyone who doesn't want *Geist* with sharp edges doesn't want *Geist* at all; not as science and not as poetry, not as art, and not as philosophy.' – FRANZ FÜHMANN, about 10 May 1933. Quoted in the *Frankfurter Rundschau*, 10 May 1993.

I was not enthusiastic when I realized (indirectly, in the form of a year-end account) that Piper Verlag possessed the rights to a paperback edition of my interview of more than two years ago with Michael Haller. Since the spring of 1991, the rapid pace of current events had certainly not slowed: the collapse of the Soviet Union with the dramatic *putsch* against Gorbachev, Yeltzin's assumption of power, the independence of the non-Russian republics, the stalled process of economic reform, and the tug-of-war in Moscow between Yeltsin and the Parliament were yet to come. The civil war in Yugoslavia had not yet broken out, and Genscher had not yet carried out his policy of an early recognition of Croatian independence. No one had yet heard of tragedies in Sarajevo or of 'ethnic cleansing' in Bosnia, and there were as yet no discussions about greater Serbian expansionism, the Vance-Owen peace plan, a Western military intervention, and so on. The Maastricht Treaty – and its rejection in Denmark, the popular vote in France, and the turbulence in England – had not yet triggered any debates on its basic principles. Bush was still sunning himself in his short-lived triumph. The old Federal Republic had not yet been overtaken by economic crisis, and the decision to move the capital from Bonn to Berlin was still ahead of us. Nobody knew where Hoyerswerda was; the asylum issue, long kept smoldering by the right-wing parties, hadn't ignited into flaming asylum shelters. I therefore advised the publisher to drop the plans for a new edition. His persistence finally moved me to read the text over again – with the result that I do not see a need for substantial revisions. Hopefully this appraisal is not attributable to an author's pigheadedness or vanity. So I present these analyses, opinions, and prognoses for a second time, expanded by a lecture on the asylum debate and the following afterword.

I

Under the influence of the recently concluded war in the Persian Gulf, discussions over the role and the legitimacy of UN operations of this kind received a great deal of attention – rightly so, as it turned out. For in the Federal Republic, as in Japan, heavy debates over participation in military operations 'out of area,' whether in Cambodia, Bosnia, or Somalia, have so far led neither to a long-overdue political decision nor to a legal-constitutional clarification. Now as in the past, the issue is not whether the military should or should not participate in 'peacemaking' as well as 'peacekeeping' measures of the UN; this distinction is in any event not razor sharp in practice. The politically decisive distinction, rather, exists between all those who take the UN's jurisdiction in the work of international peacekeeping seriously and, therefore, want to permit participation only in operations under UN command, as opposed to those who want to procure a broader political and military room for action for individual nations or unions of nations – such as NATO or the wᴇᴜ – and who thus demand the possibility of military operations 'in harmony with the ᴜɴ charter.' But Article 51 of the charter, to which this side appeals, has been abusively interpreted in the past: it served as a fig leaf for the Soviet invasion of Afghanistan, for the Falkland War, and for American attacks on Panama and Grenada. The allies' military intervention in the Persian Gulf lay somewhere in the gray area between these two sides. It was carried out under the authorization of the ᴜɴ, but under American command. For the short term, this may well be the only effective means for preventing the worst-case scenario – as in Somalia, for example. But as soon as the interests of the nations acting on behalf of the ᴜɴ are affected, a world organization that delegates its jurisdiction to others must fall under suspicion and in danger of partisanship. The German *Bundestag*, which has used alterations and new interpretations of the Basic Law to clear the way for the participation of the *Bundeswehr* in ᴜɴ operations, was supposed to have reserved the final decision for the Parliament, and to make its own consent conditional on the establishment of a standing military force under ᴜɴ command: 'The ᴜɴ already has at its disposal a legal process for the peaceful settlement of conflicts, as well as sanctions. What it lacks are organs and instruments for the effective, long-term implementation of respect for human rights, if necessary by use of force.'*

As the recent participation of units of the German air force in ᴀᴡᴀᴄs flights over Bosnia demonstrated, the administration is looking for tactical grounds to avoid such a change in the Basic Law, which could only be accomplished by working with the opposition. With the help of an all-

*R. Mutz, *Die Zeit*, 30 April 1993.

too-cooperative Federal Constitutional Court (which had
to refrain from intervening, thanks to its strongly procedur-
alistic conception of its own authority to control norms),
Kohl, Schäuble, and Rühe[1] followed an open policy of gradually militarizing our foreign policy. They trusted in the
normative force of the factual. The defense minister is under pressure from the military, which has lost sight of the
enemy and the image of the enemy, and which wants to
compensate for the military's loss of purpose by acquiring
new international theaters of operation. Moreover, even in
the face of internationally coordinated reductions in troop
strengths and the threat of the elimination of mandatory
military service (itself already lying close by reason of the
laws of war), this issue appears for the first time since 1949
to present the occasion for publicly perceptible tendencies
toward establishing the independence of the *Bundeswehr*
from the civilian leadership.

However, as is shown by the parallel course of this same
discussion in Japan, this is not the only or even the most
important context for the controversy in domestic policy
over possible 'blue-helmet' operations. Far more symptomatic for this issue is the igniting of a long-smoldering, repressed debate over the role that these two nations, simultaneously defeated and liberated from fascistic regimes in
1945, should assume in a world situation that has been radically transformed by the collapse of the Soviet Union. The
conflict, which at first was kept out of the open, concerns
how the process of adapting to the new realities should be
carried out: from the perspective of a break with the normative orientations of the post-war period, during which
Germany and Japan developed into economic powers with
noninterventionist foreign policies under the military

guardianship of the USA and NATO – or under the preserved premises of an energized recognition of that political-cultural break with the maxims and traditions that, until 1945, have stood in the way of a development of a civil society on the Western model?

At the time, I represented the position that the struggle over the opportunistic [*attentistische*] comportment of the federal government during the Gulf War would serve as a catalyst for giving fresh impetus to all those who yearned for a new 'national-state normalcy.' Since then, these revisionists and their wish for an 'uninhibited' relationship with political power – and with it the historical legacy of our *Machtpolitik* – have gotten an even bigger boost from the civil war in the former Yugoslavia. Genscher himself prepared the end of Genscherism with his policy on Croatia. Since then, the belligerent voices have been multiplying among the armchair strategists, who want to see German troops finally back on the front lines again, despite the well-grounded reservations of the military experts and in studied ignorance of the historical role of the *Wehrmacht* and the *Waffen-SS* in this region. The 'realism' of the editorial columns expresses a double wish: to exploit this situation as a way of militarily toughening up a nation that has grown unaccustomed to power, and to show off the reestablished sovereignty of a 'Great Power in the heart of Europe' towards the East. If Rühe and Kinkel – the *Plisch und Plum* of the 1990s – are tenderly feeding each other their lines, they are also orchestrating the same intertwining of military and foreign policy that once upon a time formed the backbone of sovereign states.[2]

The sovereignty of the new Germany directed toward the outside demands another kind of interior sovereignty: 'A realistic appraisal of Germany's new position by Germans themselves depends on dealing with the memories, judgments, and conceptions that have traditionally been associated with the German Great Power by others – even our neighbors and our later allies – in as sovereign a manner as possible.'* From Heinemann to Weizäcker, the maxim held true that we must remember even if others are supposed to have the chance to forget. Today, historians like Gregor Schöllgen are worried that this type of remembrance might render us incapable of assuming the international responsibilities of a European superpower. They leave no doubt as to how they imagine the new style of historical consciousness. Setting aside all the well-documented objections that the parliamentary majority had presented in the *Bundestag* debate over the location of the new capital, they confirm the worst fears of everyone who saw the wrong signal being sent with the choice of Berlin over Bonn: 'Berlin was of course also, and not least, the capital of the German Reich, the preeminent power in Europe before 1914 and once again before 1939. . . . One has to assume [!] that those in a position of political responsibility were familiar with this dimension when they chose Berlin over Bonn; that they thus consciously placed themselves within this tradition. Otherwise, the decision would be a stark example of the often-cited lack of historical consciousness, and in this sense a case of the sort of self-indulgent soul-baring [*Nabelschau*] that, in its new situation, Germany can now afford less than ever.'†

Unhappily, the birth defects of a unification process that

---

*G. Schöllgen, *Angst vor der Macht*, Berlin 1993, p.35.

†Schöllgen (1993), 31.

was administratively orchestrated and carried out according to election strategies (already discussed in the above sections of the interview) have also had long-term effects. One only needs to open the newspapers. The steelworkers' strike in the East confirms that the constitutionally derived norm of the comparability of standards of living had to open a gap between wage costs and productivity levels, which has a counterproductive effect according to the rules of a market economy. There were good reasons for overlooking foreseeable difficulties of this kind. But then, a policy of openly discussed sharing of the burden (later demanded in vain by the *Bundespräsident* as well) would have to replace the package of international treaties and naive trust in the market. Market and administrative power cannot replace solidarity – the third source of social integration – nor can a belatedly negotiated party compromise, which the Solidarity Pact cannot be, as it pretends to.[3] The recently announced resignation of the minister of transportation has a symbolic meaning that goes beyond its immediate occasion.[4] It reminds us that the treaty that Herr Schäuble, in the form of Herr Krause, made with himself had to serve as a replacement for a social contract that the citizens of both states were supposed to have worked out with one another in order to understand the conditions under which one could take responsibility for the other's welfare. What is evident today is precisely the absence of a union toward a common future made with will and consciousness.

This is precisely what the (from beginning to end hardly silent) intellectuals had in mind when they complained about the normative deficits of unification. These days (the first week of May 1993) small stories buried in the back

pages of the newspapers report what has since come of the
transfer of moral waste-products into West German management; of the politically crippled discussions over a new
constitution; of the vague appeals to dull national feeling
that go straight past the republican consciousness of a nation of citizens. Gerd Poppe reports the failure of the attempt by civil rights activists to develop broad-based 'fo-
rums for enlightenment and renewal' to cope with the past
of the GDR in their own house and under their own power;
Wolfgang Ullmann withdrew from the constitutional com-
mission with the explanation that the initiatives of the
'board of trustees for a democratically united federation of
German states' had had just as little influence on the agenda
of the negotiations as the initiatives and the petitions of
several hundred thousand citizens; the Federal Criminal
Office reports over 403 criminal acts motivated by the hatred of foreigners in March alone, among which – four
months after the deeply affecting candlelight marches – one
Turk was killed* and sixty-six people were injured.

II

Today we're busy dealing with other problems. The consequences of unification are rather grudgingly thematized
and worked out ad hoc. Normative questions yield to the
pragmatic adaptation to systemic imperatives. In domestic
policy, the political actors have drawn up a catalog of issues
that in both the West and the East corresponds to the lowest common denominator of consent. They are exactly the
kinds of issues that touch on the fears and authoritarian

---

*This was already the third death this year, coming on top of the seventeen
people killed by right-wing violence in 1992. See the report in *Stern*, 24
April 1993.

attitudes of the population and, thereby, lend grist to the mill of the *Republikaner*: asylum and foreigners, violent crime and internal security, the stability of the deutsche mark in a united Europe, drugs and nuclear-waste criminality, stemming the AIDS epidemic. Among the voting public, there is a growing feeling that these unaddressed problems are piling up because the political parties aren't even able to see the real problems, let alone handle them. The population reacts with nonparticipation in elections, with resentment against the political parties, with personalization. The substitute issues from above are matched with a substitute issue from below: corruption.

In this sense, the various political scandals are not even totted up against this or that political party; they are flatly attributed to the 'political class,' a term that has migrated into public consciousness from the jargon of the political scientists. Leaving aside Italy (where the political scandals have assumed the form of criminal prosecutions and lead one to suspect structural causes), the more or less venial sins of the politicians do not, of course, make up the phenomenon that really needs explaining. This level of corruption didn't provoke this kind of outrage during the previous several decades. The question, then, is how to explain this new sensitivity to something that has always been the case. The syndrome of growing political resentment seems to imply not just different but actually contradictory tendencies. On the one hand, there is a growing democratic indignation at the nationalization of political parties. These parties have become such an integral component of the political system that they perceive the public – from whose midst they act and whose needs they are supposed to be articulating – merely as their human surroundings, as a maneuverable mass for the creation of mass loyalty. On the other hand, there is an emerging, predemocratic anger provoked by the agonistic, circuitous, and dissonant mode in which conflicts are dragged out, and this anger reactivates old wishes for strong personalities and simple solutions. What's more, there is an objective disproportion between the limited capacities for action of the political system and the expectations that the system awakens – expectations that overburden it as long as democratic institutions don't catch up with worldwide systemic interdependencies. Whether discussed in terms of inadequate 'traction,' antidemocratic stereotypes, or limited capacities for action, all these ills have at least initially only one cure. The interlinked mobile of public communication would have to be set into play so that relevant issues and contributions, as well as agreed-upon definitions of problems and suggested solutions, can float freely, entering into public consciousness along with available information and arguments pro and con.

This has the ring of an empty formula, of course. And in fact, aren't all Western societies struggling with the same political resentments, with the same problems, with the same governments that merely push their problems ahead of themselves? The trilemma of unemployment, social-state security, and recession; the ecological limits of growth; the disparities between the essentially prosperous and peaceful industrial nations on one side and nations plagued with poverty and bloody conflicts on the other – none of these are specifically German problems. From a global perspective, one can't help but agree with Wolf Lepenies when he restores the proper perspective: our worries are the envy of the world. Of course this doesn't excuse us from the task of inspecting the disorder in our own house.

Against the background of a general malaise, one specifically German feature does stand out: our political parties
have piled up problems where they didn't need to. This is
just as true of the scurrilous treatment of the question of
blue-helmet operations as it is for the questions of asylum
and immigration, which were yanked from public discussion with a slapdash and still-contested party compromise
at the first whiff of sulfur from the right. The same holds
true for the question of developing the EC into a political
union: while our political parties were publicly beating
around the bush, other countries were holding public refer-
enda. And finally, it's true for the economic but above all the
social consequences of unification, which the government
answered with a hand-to-mouth policy. All these problems
persist within a peculiar *claire-obscure*. The opposition is
clearly neither willing nor able to set the obvious alternatives out for discussion in a broadly effective manner.

I have already mentioned the alternatives regarding the
issue of military operations 'out of area.' Unless we merely
want to expand the capacity of individual nations or regional alliances to participate in worldwide military interventions 'in harmony' with the UN charter, we have to contribute to the creation of an effective world institution with
the aim of making the UN capable of enforcing its own resolutions, on its own if necessary, with units under its own
command. On the issue of foreigners, an alternative to the
negotiated party compromise has to insist on the following
points. First, the 'essential content' of an individual's legal
claim to political asylum may not be undermined, whether
by making arrangements with 'secure third states' or with
one-sided definitions of 'persecution-free states.' Second,
the argument that we are not a nation of immigrants con-

tradicts the historical facts. Third, there is a link between the issue of political asylum and those economically motivated migration movements that need to be channeled with fair legislation on immigration. This is why our immigration laws need to be transferred to the principle of territory, in order to simplify the naturalization of foreigners who are already settled here (also under the condition of dual citizenship.)

As far as the issue of Europe's future is concerned, we need to say what the alternatives *are not*: they are not a choice between the economic-liberal continuation down the chosen path or the national-conservative demonization of the 'Maastricht Monster.' The opponents to a European currency union want to keep the deutsche mark functioning as a benchmark currency, as a way of politically exploiting our regained national sovereignty within the bounds of an eastwardly expanded, but politically rather loosely integrated, European Community. A decisive democratization of the Brussels-based EC is the only convincing alternative to this backward-looking effort of assuring for Germany – on its third try – the position as the preeminent European power at the heart of the continent. A Community developed along federalist lines and expanded to include the European Free Trade Association must not only preserve the historical and cultural singularities of individual nations; it must also tap them as sources of vital, yet interconnected, political public spheres. This is the only basis for the existence of the Strasbourg Parliament, and for its ability to support broad-based institutions that in turn would give the communicative power of citizens a chance to steer the systemic operations of the Common Market. Only a substantially democratic European constitution – one that is more than a legal-administrative arrangement of market mechanisms – could put to rest the normative reservations of the former Federal Constitutional Court justices Benda, Hesse, and Simon,* as well as their colleague Dieter Grimm.†

These points of view are neither new nor particularly exciting. What, then, is preventing the effective public thematization of these problems under clear alternatives? My suspicion is that this isn't happening because the alternatives I have named cannot help but evoke a deeper, still repressed controversy. Since 1989, a process of self-understanding of citizens concerning the role of their expanded republic has been lacking. Nevertheless, even after the quickly squelched attempts at a constitutional discussion, there are still mutterings of this process behind the scenes. The question, then, is under which categories will the new situation be understood? Some maintain that historians in particular are now called on 'to give a competent answer to the question of the status of the new Germany in the world.'‡ And at the same time they want to replace the analytical perspective of social history and the social sciences with the concretistic vision of spatial and temporal shifts. A geopolitical shift of the Federal Republic from the 'peripheral position' back into the old 'continental central position' also suggests a new punctuation of the historical past: 'Despite the "westward shift" of the postwar period, the new Germany must become far more similar to the old

---

*Cf. *Die Zeit*, 26 June 1992.

†In *Merkur*, December 1992, pp.1059–76.

‡Schollgen (1993), 177.

Germany than the divided nations FRG and GDR.'* From this point of view, the historical turning points themselves undergo a shift: the time period between 1917 and 1989, which we can now finally see past, is bundled up as the 'epoch of global civil war,' and within it the period from 1933 to 1945 shrinks to a single episode. Behind the celebrations of the historical break of 1989 there hides the perpetually frustrated desire for normalization of those for whom the historical break of 1945 was always burdensome. In this way, the alternative behind the alternatives, which until recently the political public sphere always shied away from, now steps into the light: should the expanded Federal Republic continue down the chosen path of political civilization, or is the old special consciousness going to renew itself in a different form? Both the transformed constellation of world powers and a changed internal situation certainly demand new responses. The question is only in what kind of consciousness the Federal Republic will complete the course of adaptation. We need clarity on this, especially if, in view of the fourth issue, the consequences of unification, things are not simply to remain in the old pattern of reactions of ad hoc decisions and subcutaneous moods.

III

Why has the debate on self-understanding not gotten going? Surely the conservative parties don't regard themselves as being unequal to the intellectual task of sparking arguments on basic political questions. They subtly move the goal posts from case to case; time and the Zeitgeist are working in their favor. Now that the eastward shift of the

*K. Weissmann, *Rückruf in die Geschichte*, Berlin 1992, p.192.

capital has produced some quieting 'facts,' it's no accident
that the lame discussions over what had been planned as
the Bonn memorial to the dead of the Second World War
now continues as a purely aesthetic argument.*

Of course, this doesn't explain why the opposition is
so helpless that they let the baiting tactics of the Rühes,
Schäubles, and Seiters force them into the role of partners
of the right. Nor does a reference to the ideological decay of
the socialist parties help much further; after the collapse of
the Soviet Union, absolutely nothing was left over apart
from the ecologically expanded social-democratic programmatic. One is more likely to find an explanation from
the intellectual scene, where all the fronts have become
confused, than from the political parties themselves.

*The argument concerns whether the Schinckelian Watch, as redesigned
by Tessenov, should be augmented with the Christian (!) gestures of the
Kollwitz Madonna, or whether this site, owing to the unspeakable inter-
twinings of fates during the Second World War, is capable of tolerating
only an abstract, inscriptionless configuration. Thus the real question –
why the Holocaust Memorial is in Washington and not Berlin – is utterly
lost sight of. And the basic question of whether the political language of
such a memorial – into which, indeed, the link with the collective of the
Germans is gramatically inscribed – is at all capable of the required ab-
straction, is never even raised at all. Only from the distance of a universalistic perspective – in the face of God, if such a formulation is permitted
in a postreligious society – would the political-moral differences between
culprits and victims, between 'victims' of one kind or another, between the
war dead and the resistance fighters, between the murderers, the collaborators, and the murdered, be indifferent [*gleichgultig*]. Only the state of
Israel can memorialize its victims unambiguously; under other presuppositions, every nationally sponsored collective memorial at least carries
the suggestion with it that a commanded *sacrificium* is being consecrated
for questionable ends. This runs up against the maxim of the 'elimination
of the victim' (Adorno) that, after the barbarities of the twentieth century,
must at least be clear to us.

Here the bankruptcy of state socialism and the lifting of
the Iron Curtain even had an initially positive effect in the
context of struggles over domestic policy issues. The ubiq-
uitous distrust of internal enemies of the state, which had
been dominant for forty years, has become objectless, and
this has detoxified the atmosphere. The Carl Schmitt–
inspired Great Suspicion of the subversive left has nothing
left to feed on. The left, for its part, has become pragmatic.
Even the hackneyed, cure-all formula calling for the social
and ecological 'taming' of capitalism is accepted on all sides
in its strong reading as a 'reconfiguration' of industrial society. Now that the struggle over property forms has (long
since) lost its dogmatic meaning, the contest of political
ideas has shifted broadly from the level of social-political
goals to the level of their operationalization.* Nevertheless,
the old camps are still in their trenches – or just changing
sides. The neoconservatives and their grandchildren are
still mulling over the question of 'What's Left';[5] they can't
seem to tear themselves away from the worn-out melodies
of a critique of utopia that the left itself looked after for a
long time. As Andre Gorz has written, 'If the right con-
demns every guiding idea, every vision of the future that
rises above the level of Realpolitik as a dangerous utopia,
then they are contributing to the emergence of a vacuum
that is being filled by the extreme right-wing utopias of
camaraderie, order, and discipline in the total state. A right
that fights against the supposed shadow of Sovietism in
every left runs the risk of being overrun by the right itself.'
(*Frankfurter Allgemeine Zeitung*, 17 March 1993). In other

---

*J. Habermas, 'Nachholende Revolution und linker Revisionsbedarf,' in
ders (1992), pp.213–41.

words, entirely new fronts are forming within the right which, by the simplistic division of the world into global civil war parties [*Weltburgerkriegsparteien*] has lost its un-reflective orientation.

If the left nevertheless refuses the imposed break [*Soll-bruchstelle*] of a 'normalization' fueled by the right – if it behaves rather tentatively, instead of demanding a missing 'realignment' – this may have something to do with the heavy demands that have been placed on it by a change of roles. We are not accustomed to the literally conservative role that we assume as we throw our support behind the continuation of a process of civilization, of culturally turn-ing to the West, that was introduced with the old Federal Republic, or if we think back to all the old problems that haven't been solved by recent events. I mean those prob-lems that the SPD had already tried to tackle in its Berlin program, which was so quickly run over by the wheels of nation.

What's more, this view of things doesn't exactly make the desired dialogue between western and eastern intellectuals any easier. Here, it seems, the misunderstanding inevitably arises that the debate over self-understanding should still be run according to the same familiar pattern of entrance, annexation, and liquidation – provided Wolf Lepenies's di-agnosis is not entirely false, at any rate: 'In the Federal Re-public, the early internationalization of many disciplines and scientific areas . . . itself forced by persecution, emigra-tion, and repatriation, brought about a very early cultural "Westward orientation" that anticipated the integration into a Western alliance, and later on decisively contributed to its inner stability. . . . In the West, the stock of spiritual tradi-tions internationalized themselves, and many elements of cultural self-understanding were de-Germanized. In the East they sang the International under duress and remained provincial. The socialistic GDR became a reserve of German interiority. . . . In the German State of Farmers and Workers, for a very long time, no literary critic [could] freely read, teach, and communicate Kafka, no philosopher Wittgenstein, no psychologist Sigmund Freud. Within the territory of the former GDR, which so prized itself as a nation of readers, artistic and scientific methods were barred over the course of a half-century – here we can draw the years from 1933 to 1989 into one timespan.'* Even under these premises, there is a common basis for understanding, of course: 'The unified Germany could also find a shared political-moral orientation by reappropriating the antifascism of the early GDR.'†

Of course, antifascism was so instrumentalized by the SED, so damaged in its moral substance, that it forms the backdrop against which a reborn intellectual right wing can present itself as a pristine, visionary force with new answers at the ready for the new situation. This gesture – a simultaneous repulsion and a need to surpass – had quite early been expressed with the formula that history has 'voted out' the '68ers. Since then, the avant-garde gestures from the right have developed into a visible sign for a mental attitude that binds a great many things together – from the Freiburg student newspaper 'Young Freedom' all the way to Rainer Zitelmann's contemporary program in the noble Ullstein Press. Ironically, these enterprises give the title 'The Past as Future' a fresh new meaning: at closer inspection, they re-

*W. Lepenies, *Folgen einer unerhörten Begebenheit*, Berlin 1992, 72f.

†Lepenies (1992), 74.

veal themselves to be the third rehashing of the ideas of a young-conservative group of intellectuals who, after 1945, remained politically incoherent and were left out in the cold; at any rate, with their resentment that developed in the early postwar period they could only reach intellectuals in the vicinity of Armin Mohler or Bernard Willms. The just-published notes of Carl Schmitt from the time imme-diately after the end of the war, in which he complains of 'terror from Nazis and Jews,' gives Lepenies occasion for the dry commentary: 'All traditions can be reactivated. In Ger-many today people are speaking in plain language again.'

IV

How this looks can be read in Karl-Heinz Weissmann. He too reverses the special path [*Sonderweg*] hypothesis and dismisses the old Federal Republic – along with its rein-terpretation of the defeat of 1945 into a liberation and its predominating consciousness of 'a people refuted by his-tory' – as a more or less pathological interim. Today, the patriotically minded intelligentsia thus stand before the task of a new national education, and Weissmann explains to the nation why the Germans deserve a 'return to nor-malcy' both from themselves and from their neighbors. In this way, Ernst Nolte's thesis on the end of the global civil war is enriched and granted variety by the legacy of Carl Schmitt in the style of the 1950s.

Since 1917 – initially with Wilson and Lenin as exponents – the utopian projects of World Democracy and World Rev-olution have confronted each other. Both were products of the Enlightenment. To the extent that these large abstrac-tions developed historical dynamics, history lost its natural rhythm. World civil war caused history (which was infected, so to speak, with the bacillus of the philosophy of history) to derail. History was wrenched from its ground. Only in 1989 did it return back to its normal aggregate state: Leningrad is once again St. Petersburg. Consistently, Weissmann interprets the new eruptions of national conflicts as signs of normalization: 'If we are entering into a stage of Balkanization after the end of the empires of the twentieth century, then history is following one of its very few truly recognizable laws.'* In this way, too, the losers of 1945 also reenter their 'historical existence.' They must again become the subject of a more or less social-Darwinistic *Machtpolitik*. Above all, they must free themselves from the *Vergangenheitsbewältigung* imposed on them from the outside.

Now the Nazi period appears as an unfortunate sidetrack of a process of world civil war – a war whose predetermined battle lines could only be drawn after 1945, because Stalin and Roosevelt didn't identify each other as the true adversaries in a timely way. What one could call the misleading wartime coalition against Hitler is explicable by the geopolitically conditioned encircling of a delayed nation. In the end, 'the German tragedy is grounded in the fact that, in the last phase of the "Thirty Years War" [clearly being dated by setting 1914 as its beginning], a struggle for national existence and global civil war lay indistinguishably superimposed on one another. The desperate attempts of the leadership of the *Wehrmacht* to hold the eastern front, to allow the population to flee from the advancing Red Army, and Hitler's "Nero commands," with which he tried to punish the people for their "failure," show both aspects up to their final consequences.'†

*Weissmann (1992), 75.

†Weissmann (1992), 89f.

Some obvious inferences follow once history has been whipped into shape in this way: a rejection of Europe goes hand in hand with the view eastwards, since 'the old core provinces of the German East (i.e., East Prussia, Silesia, and the eastern parts of Pomerania and Brandenburg) have been utterly untouched by the reunification of the rest of the states.'

A revisionist view of the world, whether in this or in a more moderate variety, stands or falls with the presupposition that the nation remains the proper size and shape for the identity of modern states. In Weissmann's words, 'The nation will remain the constitutive order for as long as the planet exists as a *pluriversum*.'* This thesis, which seems to meet with such general agreement today, is in no way supported by current evidence. What Weissmann judges as Balkanization is the dominion of the past over the future.

It is certainly true that a collective that understands itself as a community with its own identity gains a new level of acknowledgment with the step towards statehood – a level that was denied to it as a pre-political, linguistic, and ethnic community. The need for acknowledgment as a nation-state is even stronger in times of crisis, especially if (as was the case after the dissolution of the Soviet empire) the population clings to the ascriptive features of a regressively renovated collective identity. But even in the face of social instability and deep anxieties about the future, the compensations that this hold on collective identity promise are all very dubious. The nations that appear to build the foundations of nation-states are all highly artificial constructs. They are fictive unities, the results of violent processes of

*Weissmann (1992), 135.

homogenization. The historical formation of nation-states shows that new national minorities emerge with the drawing of new national boundaries; the old problems don't disappear even at the cost of 'ethnic cleansing.'

In Western Europe, in any event, things are different. The multiculturalism that has formed here under the pressure of worldwide migration movements is a necessity, not an option. On the way to a European Union, the existing nation-states themselves are the actual problem. The frictions that they cause in this process only confirm the overburdening of nation-states' capacity to act in a world of growing systemic interdependencies. The twenty-first century confronts us with challenges to which the classical nation-states themselves aren't adequate. In his newest book, Paul Kennedy has investigated five large trends: the asymmetrically divided, explosive growth of human population; the biotechnological transformation of agricultural production; the computer-guided automatization of industrial production; the electronic coordination of financial markets and the emergence of multinational corporations; and finally the increasing ecological exhaustion of the natural environment. It is no accident that his analyses all head toward one single point: the future of the nation-state: For many population groups, it appears to have become 'the *wrong sort* of unit to handle the newer circumstances. For some problems, it is too large to operate effectively; for others, it is too small. In consequence, there are pressures for a "relocation of authority" both upward and downward, creating structures that might respond better to today's and tomorrow's forces for change.'* For this reason, today's

---

*Paul Kennedy, *Preparing for the Twenty-first Century* (New York: Random House, 1993), 131.

agenda is calling for the creation of more complex unities through the simultaneous democratization of existing political institutions. Only if the forces of democratic constitutional states can be bound together into larger political unities such as a European Union; only if regional, effective conferences and alliances can be created between states; only if the United Nations can be transformed from a resolutionary to an acting committee – only then does the chance still exist that citizens can, in full consciousness and with their own will, assume influence upon the development of worldwide systemic operations through their own political public spheres and their own democratic conduct.

What was once meant by the idea of popular sovereignty is doomed to decay into a mere chimera if it remains locked in the historical form of the self-asserting, sovereign nation-state. But the political actors lose the feel for the obstinacy of the normative just as quickly in the European arena as they do in the sphere of internal affairs. The emancipatory meaning of constitutional norms grows pale in light of supposedly factual constraints and systemic imperatives.

Translator's Notes

PREFACE

1. See Jürgen Habermas, 'The New Obscurity: The Crisis of the Welfare State and the Exhaustion of Utopian Energies,' in Jürgen Habermas, *The New Conservatism: Cultural Criticism and the Historians' Debate*, ed. and trans. Shierry Weber Nicholsen (Cambridge, MA: MIT Press, 1989), 48–70.

THE GULF WAR

1. Micha Brumlek: Professor of Education at the University of Heidelberg and a major contributor to the 'Historians' Debate' in 1986–87. See his article on German unification, 'Basic Aspects of an Imaginary Debate,' *New German Critique* 52 (Winter 1991): 102–9.

2. Hans-Magnus Enzensberger: author, essayist, poet, prominent figure of the West German left, and member of the 'Group 47' movement along with Günter Grass and Heinrich Böll.

3. Jean-François Lyotard: prolific French philosopher of the 'postmodern condition.' His most recent works in English include *Toward the Postmodern* (Atlantic Highlands, N.J.: Humanities Press, 1993) and *Political Writings* (Minneapolis: University of Minnesota Press, 1993). For Habermas's views on Lyotard and postmodernism, see *The Philosophical Discourse of Modernity* (Cambridge, MA: MIT Press). Karl-Heinz Bohrer: professor of literature at Bielefeld University and editor of the journal *Merkur*. Bohrer was highly critical of left intellectual objections to German unification and advocated the need for a recovery of German nationhood. See Karl-Heinz Bohrer, 'Warum wir kein Nation sind: Warum wir eine werden sollen,' *Frankfurter Allgemeine Zeitung*, 13 January 1990; the essay appears in English translation as 'Why We Are Not a Nation – And Why We Should Become One,' in *When the Wall Came Down: Reactions to German Unification*, ed. Harold James and Marla Stone (New York: Routledge, 1992), 60–70.

4. Carl Friedrich von Weisäcker: nuclear physicist, peace activist, and brother of *Bundespräsident* Richard von Weisäcker.

5. Historians' Debate: touched off in 1985 by Helmut Kohl's visit to the Bitburg cemetery and by Federal president Richard von Weisäcker's moving speech to the *Bundestag* on the fortieth anniversary of Germany's surrender at the end of World War II. The Historians' Debate pitted conservative historians such as Ernst Nolte, Andreas Hillgruber, and Joachim Fest against their liberal counterparts. Citing Germany's responsibilities as a part of the Western anticommunist alliance, the conservatives insisted that the 'burden of the past' be eased; Nolte went so far as to insist that this unburdening could be helped by recognizing that the Holocaust was merely a 'distorted copy' of the Soviet gulag. Leftist historians and political scientists, Habermas prominent among them, argued that these relativizing arguments served to instrumentalize Germans' moral confrontation with their own past in the name of short-term political strategies. Most of Habermas's contributions to the Historians' Debate have been translated in *The New Conservatism: Cultural Criticism and the Historians' Debate*, ed. and trans. Shierry Weber Nicholsen (Cambridge, MA: MIT Press, 1989).

6. *Steuerlüge*: literally 'tax lie'; the Kohl administration's pledge to finance the enormous costs of German unification without raising taxes.

7. David Grossman: Israeli journalist and novelist, best known for his accounts of the Israeli-Palestinian conflict. His most recent book is *Sleeping on a Wire: Conversations with Palestinians in Israel* (New York: Farrar, Straus & Giroux, 1993).

8. Yorim Kaniuk: one of Israel's most influential contemporary novelists. Kaniuk's most recent works include *Confessions of a Good Arab* (London: Haliban, 1987) and *His Daughter* (London: Haliban, 1988).

9. Ernst Tugendhat: professor of philosophy at the Free University of Berlin.

10. In Karl-Otto Apel, *Diskurs und Verantwortung* (Frankfurt: Suhrkamp, 1988), 370ff.

11. WEU: Compromise mutual defense organization introduced in 1954 by the Eden Plan, the WEU set the terms for the postwar rearma-

ment of the Federal Republic and the conditions for its entrance into NATO.

12. Genscherism: Hans-Dietrich Genscher, longtime leader of the West German Free Democrat Party (FDP) and foreign minister of the Federal Republic from 1974 to 1992 in both the Schmidt and Kohl administrations. As foreign minister, Genscher followed a policy emphasizing pragmatism, careful consensus building, and multilateral arrangements in all significant foreign policies, in order to bind West Germany into multinational alliances and avoid isolation.

13. *Tatkreise*: circle of right-wing intellectuals associated with Hans Zehrer's journal *Die Tat* (The Deed), an important literary forum for the 'conservative revolution' in the closing days of the Weimar Republic.

14. Karl-Heinz Bohrer, 'Provinzialismus (II). Ein Psychogram,' in *Merkur* 45 (1991), 255 –62.

THE NORMATIVE DEFICITS

1. 'Old boys' network': the German, *alte Seilschaften*, is borrowed from mountain climbing; a *Seilschaft* is a team of climbers on a single rope – figuratively, they either hang together or hang separately.

2. Konrad Weiss: leading spokesman of the Democracy Now movement in the fall of 1989; together with the New Forum, Democracy Now was the most significant oppositional citizens' movement in the GDR prior to unification. The activities of the New Forum and Democracy Now were an important catalyst for the revolution that toppled the SED regime. Friedrich Schorlemmer: Protestant pastor and cofounder, with Edelbert Richter, of the Democratic Awakening party. Schorlemmer is currently a member of the SPD. Bischof Forck: prominent oppositional clergyman whose public reflections on the role of the church in the GDR was an important impetus for Democracy Now in the late 1980s. Bärbel Bohley: artist and (according to the Stasi) 'mother of the underground'; the best-known figure in the East German opposition in the 1980s, and founder, in the fall of 1989, of the New Forum.

3. FDJ: *Freie Deutsche Jugend* (Free German Youth), the official youth

organization of the SED (see note 5 below). DEFA Films: Founded in 1946, the Deutsche Film AG (German Film, Inc.) was the largest and most influential state-operated producer of motion pictures in East Germany. Throughout the late 1940s and particularly in the 1950s, DEFA specialized in rigidly realistic antifascist parables. Many of DEFA's products were of extremely high quality (*The Murderers among Us* [1946] was postwar Germany's first internationally successful film). Moreover, the earlier DEFA films often dealt directly and powerfully with Germany's Nazi past and its contemporary social problems at a time when West German culture was producing nothing comparable.

4. Friedrichstraße subway station: the single subway stop between East and West Berlin, extraordinarily heavily guarded and patrolled.

5. SED: The *Sozialistische Einheitspartei Deutschlands* (German Socialist Unity Party), the ruling communist party of the GDR.

6. See Georg Lukács, *Die Zerstörung der Vernunft* (East Berlin: Aufbau Verlag, 1956).

7. Markus Wolf: until 1986 the head of the GDR's intelligence; as East Germany's spymaster, Wolf was also an important mouthpiece for the Soviet Union in the final days of the SED regime and played an important role in the effort to force the resignation of Erich Honecker. After serving as a member of Gregor Gysi's consultive committee in 1990, Wolf fled to the Soviet Union before German unification. Fleeing the Soviet Union after the failed coup against Michail Gorbachev, Wolf was arrested at the German border in September 1991. Charged with numerous civil and human rights violations, Wolf went on trial before a federal court in the summer of 1993.

8. Lothar de Maizière, chairman of the East German CDU, was elected minister president of the GDR in 1990. After unification in October 1990 de Maizière served as a minister without portfolio in the Kohl administration, and in December 1990 was elected as a representative in the *Bundestag* for the new state of Brandenburg. Before the year's end, however, de Maizière was obliged to resign all his public offices under mounting evidence that he had served as an informant for the Stasi.

9. Bloc parties: the SED and its state-controlled, ornamental 'opposition' parties – the East German CDU, the LDP, NDP, and the National Peasant Party – which in practice acted as a self-sustaining bloc in the Politburo-engineered elections.

10. In May 1990 the finance ministers of East and West Germany signed a treaty mandating the economic unification of the two Germanies; the treaty called for an exchange rate of 1:1 between the West German deutsche mark and the greatly less valuable East German mark. Soon after the treaty on economic unity took effect in July, the de Maizière government agreed to parliamentary elections in the five East German states in October, and an all-German election for December 1990, thus de facto forfeiting the sovereignty of the GDR.

11. Dreggerian consciousness: reference to Alfred Dregger, representative of the extreme right wing of the CDU.

12. Claus Offe: professor of political science and sociology at the University of Bremen.

13. Round Table: In December 1989, amid the collapse of the SED regime, the Round Table was established as an informal group composed of representatives from the recently legalized oppositional parties and last representatives of the SED, most notably Gregor Gysi, who replaced Egon Krenz as general secretary of the SED on 6 December. In the political vacuum created by the collapse of the communist party, the Round Table proposed to coalesce into a political entity with the self-proclaimed responsibility of ensuring democratic practices on the part of Minister President Hans Modrow's interim government until the March 1991 elections in the *Volkskammer* and the creation of a draft constitution for the post-SED East German government.

14. Oskar Lafontaine: Social Democrat prime minister of Saarland and chancellor candidate, Lafontaine is the leading representative of the pragmatic-moderate wing of the SPD. Lafontaine argued strongly in 1990 against an accelerated unification process in favor of a gradualist and indefinite intermingling of the two Germanies, leading toward a 'third way' between bureaucratic state socialism and capitalism.

15. In March 1990 Habermas published an essay in *Die Zeit* entitled

'Der DM-Nationalismus'; a longer version appeared in *New German Critique* (Winter 1991) and is reprinted in James and Stone, *When the Wall Came Down,* 86–102, as 'Yet Again: German Identity – a Unified Nation of Angry DM-Burghers.' There, Habermas remarked that 'the renewed national consciousness would no longer make up for the burdens of a capitalist modernization that is nevertheless also cushioned by social-welfare measures; a national consciousness that found its symbolic expression in the strength of the D-Mark would, on the contrary, be forced to ignore the voice of enlightened self-interest, pushing the skeptical economic Burgher to collective efforts and sacrifices *in his own language*' (91).

16. Article 23 of the West German Basic Law guarantees the validity of the Basic Law in 'other parts' of Germany upon their entrance to the Federal Republic; in effect, it provides a simple means for the admission of new states into the *Bundesrepublik*. The framers of the Basic Law had intended Article 23 to apply principally to the Saarland, which entered the Federal Republic by this means in 1957. Kohl's *Deutschlandpolitik,* and the 'Alliance for Germany' engineered by the federal government for the March 1990 East German parliamentary elections, both strongly emphasized the appeal to Article 23 as a speedy and uncomplicated constitutional medium for the unification process, inasmuch as it would not require any change in the (West German) Basic Law itself. Article 146, however, sought to establish the provisional nature of the Basic Law – that is, the difference between the Basic Law and a constitution – by stipulating that 'this Basic Law loses its validity on the day that a new constitution takes effect, concluded by the German people in free decision.' During the unification process itself, Habermas had strongly argued that the Kohl administration's studied ignorance of the provision for a constitutional convention according to Article 146 deprived the German people of the very chance for collective self-determination that was at the normative heart of the Basic Law itself: in the March 1990 essay 'Yet Again: German Identity: A Nation of Angry DM-Burghers,' Habermas wrote that

identification with the principles and the institutions of our constitution demands . . . an agenda for reunification which gives priority to the freely exercised right of the citizens to

determine their own future by direct vote, within the framework of a non-occupied public sphere that has not already
been willed away. This means, concretely, that the will of the
voting public is given precedence over an annexation cleverly initiated but in the final analysis carried through only at
the administrative level – an annexation which dishonestly
evades one of the essential conditions for the founding of any
nation of state-citizens: the public act of a carefully considered democratic decision taken in both parts of Germany.
This act of foundation can only be carried out consciously
and intentionally if we agree not to accomplish unification
via Art. 23 of our Basic Law. (96)

17. '2 + 4 Treaty': the agreement of 12 September 1990 that constituted
the official international settlement of German division, thereby
formally ending the conflict of World War II. In the ten articles of
the treaty, West and East Germany (2) agreed both with each other
and with the wartime allies the United States, Great Britain, France,
and the Soviet Union (+ 4) on terms for the unification of the two
German states.

18. The reference is to Andreas Kuhlmann, 'Nachgeholte Legitimation,' *Frankfurter Allgemeine Zeitung,* 19 December 1990.

19. According to West German election laws, voters are accorded two
ballots in federal elections, the 'first vote' cast for a candidate in a
local constituency, the 'second vote' for a list of candidates presented by a political party. In the 1953 elections, Gustav Heinemann, who had withdrawn from Konrad Adenauer's cabinet in
protest over the rearmament question, formed the GVP, a short-
lived pacifist party. Heinemann later migrated to the SPD and was
elected *Bundespräsident* in 1969. Kurt Schumacher, leader of the
SPD until his death in 1952, was an early critic of Adenauer's reconstruction and West-oriented policies, and an advocate of a speedy
recovery of German unity.

20. Konrad Adenauer, first chancellor of the Federal Republic, decided early on in the process of the reconstruction of Germany that
it would be impossible to exclude all former members of the Nazi
party ('Pg's') from the ranks of government and administration.
During the early 1950s Adenauer vigorously pushed for a program

of rearmament for the Federal Republic on the grounds of its enhanced responsibility as the front line against Soviet aggression in middle Europe, hoping that the remilitarization question could be used as leverage to extract assurances of West German sovereignty from the wartime allies.

21. In the summer of 1990 East German interior minister Peter-Michael Diestel refused public access to the vast surveillance files accumulated over decades by the Stasi; the draft unification treaty written over the course of that summer provided for the transfer of those files into West Germany, where they would be made available to intelligence services. The public outcry over this eventuality led to demonstrations, sit-ins, and hunger strikes at the former Stasi headquarters and, in September, to a compromise agreement, according to which the files would remain on site, but off limits to citizens. They remain there to this day.

22. See Günter Grass, 'Short Speech by a Rootless Cosmopolitan' (1990) and 'Writing after Auschwitz' (1990), in *Two States – One Nation?,* trans. Krishna Winston and A. S. Wensinger (New York: Harcourt Brace Jovanovich, 1990).

23. Alliance for Germany: the unlikely campaign alliance, engineered and supported by the Kohl administration, that captured a surprising 48 percent of the vote in the March 1990 parliamentary elections in East Germany. The 'Alliance for Germany' was composed of the East German CDU, headed by Lothar de Maizière, the popular organization Democratic Awakening, and the DSU (Deutsche Soziale Union, the 'German Social Union'), the right-wing offshoot of the CSU, the CDU's Bavarian affiliate.

24. Otto Schily, an attorney who argued the defense of the Baader-Meinhof gang in the 1960s, later a prominent figure in the pragmatic 'realo' wing of the West German Green party. In 1989 Schily switched from the Greens to the SPD. The reference is to 'banana freedom,' a term that many West Germans, Schily included, sardonically observed in their East German neighbors who, as they streamed into West Berlin in November 1989, expressed their enthusiasm not so much for the institutions and principles of democratic rule as for bananas, which were unavailable in the East, and which the newly liberated 'Ossis' consumed in prodigious quantities.

25. Theodor Waigel, conservative leader of the CSU and since 1989 minister of finance.

THE PAST AS FUTURE

1. Otto Graf Lambsdorff, prominent Free Democrat and formerly Kohl's economics minister; resigned in 1984 after being implicated of accepting bribes in the Flick affair.

2. 'Two-thirds society': a society in which the structural constraints of capitalism can provide economic well-being only to two-thirds of the population.

3. Berlin Plan: calling for unilateral nuclear disarmament and the resulting dismantling of NATO.

4. That is, a coalition of the SPD and the West German Green party.

5. See Joachim Fest, 'Schwiegende Wortführer: Überlegungen zu einer Revolution ohne Vorbild,' *Frankfurter Allgemeine Zeitung*, 30 December 1989. The essay has been translated as 'The Silence of the Clerks' in Harold James and Marla Stone, eds., *When the Wall Came Down: Reactions to German Unification* (New York: Routledge, 1992), 52–56.

6. Antje Vollmer, MP and spokesperson for the Green party in the Federal *Bundestag*.

7. Sir Ralf Dahrendorf: historian and political scientist. He has been a member of the West German parliament, a cabinet minister, the commissioner of the European Community, and the director of the London School of Economics. He is currently warden of Saint Anthony's College, Oxford. For Dahrendorf's views on developments in Europe see *Reflections on the Revolution in Europe* (New York: Random House, 1990).

8. *Vormärz*: period from 1815 until the March revolution of 1848, in which the German states struggled for national unity according to essentially liberal political principles.

9. Andrew Arato: professor of sociology at the New School for Social Research, New York.

10. The title of Habermas's most recent anthology of political essays. See Jürgen Habermas, *Die Nachholende Revolution: Kleine Politische Schriften VII* (Frankfurt: Suhrkamp Verlag, 1990).

11. Wolf Biermann: poet and singer, East Germany's most prominent dissident until his expulsion in 1976. The reference is to his works

Preußischer Ikarus (Cologne: Kiepenheuer & Witsch, 1978) and *Der Sturz des Daedalus*.

12. In 1990 Christa Wolf, East Germany's most prominent writer, published a short book that she had written in 1979. *Was Bleibt* (*What Remains*) is a quiet and agonizing account of her surveillance and harrassment by the East German Stasi from 1976 to 1979. In the summer of 1990 two reviews – one by Ulrich Greiner, the other by Frank Schirrmacher – criticized Christa Wolf's decision to rewrite and publish her book only after the fall of the SED regime had removed the threat of official disapproval. Greiner's critique of Wolf was particularly harsh, accusing her of accommodating herself to the SED regime, lacking the moral courage for forthright dissidence, and enjoying the perks and privileges accorded to her as East Germany's most prominent writer, thus in effect earning an undeserved reputation as the 'conscience of the DDR.' The attack unleashed a furious debate about the future of literature in the former East Germany and the moral *Vergangenheitsbewältigung* of the East German republic, and gave a wrenching preview of the moral, cultural, and political wounds and problems that lie ahead for the unified Germany. After months of conspicuous silence, Wolf entered a kind of self-imposed exile in California in 1992; the *Literaturstreit* reached its sad denouement in February 1993, when she quietly acknowledged that, like so many of her colleagues, she too had served as an informant for the Stasi (see *Der Spiegel*, 25 January 1993). Excerpts of Wolf's *What Remains* were published in *Granta* 33. For a thorough account of the political ramifications of the 'Literature Controversy' see Andreas Huyssen, 'After the Wall: The Failure of German Intellectuals,' in *New German Critique* 52 (Winter 1991): 109–43.

13. The reference is to the cultural feuilleton of the *Frankfurter Allgemeine Zeitung*.

14. Peter Rühmkorf: noted poet and literary critic.

15. Ivan Nagel: professor of aesthetics and art history at the Hochschüle der Kunst in Berlin.

16. The currency reform of 1948 introduced the deutsche mark as a replacement for the German reichsmark. The immediate popularity of the DM was a crucial first step in the economic recovery of

postwar Germany. The Soviet Union's vigorous objection to the introduction of the DM without their approval was a major contributing factor leading to the Berlin Blockade of 1948.

17. H. A. Winckler: professor of modern history at the University of Freiburg, noted historian of the Weimar Republic, and participant in the Historians' Debate in 1986–87.

EUROPE'S SECOND CHANCE

1. 'Catching up and overtaking' (*Einholen und Überholen*): East German slogan promising higher levels of industrial production and social security than in West Germany.

2. Francis Fukuyama, neoconservative political theorist and former US State Department official, whose widely discussed article 'The End of History' employed Hegelian categories to diagnose the collapse of communism and the historical victory of capitalist democracies. See Fukuyama's more recent book, *The End of History and the Last Man* (New York: Free Press, 1992).

3. Christian Meier: professor of ancient history at the University of Munich. Meier has written extensively on German nationhood and was a prominent participant in the Historians' Debate.

4. See Ernst Bloch, *Natural Law and Human Dignity,* trans. Dennis J. Schmidt (Cambridge, MA: MIT Press, 1986), xxix.

5. Adam Michnik, a Polish historian and journalist, was a leading dissident and organizer of the KOR (Committee for the Defense of Workers); his best-known publication is *Letters from Prison and Other Essays*. He is currently the editor of Warsaw's daily *Gazeta Wyborcza* and a deputy in Poland's parliament. For his views on German unification and Poland, see his article 'Opportunity Rather Than a Threat,' in James and Stone, *When the Wall Came Down*, 327–28.

6. Trust Company (*Treuhandgesellschaft*): government agency charged with the reconstruction of the economy of the former GDR, including decisions concerning the privatization or liquidation of thousands of inviable and cash-poor industries.

7. Adam Przeworski: Polish historian and economist. His most recent work is *Democracy and the Market: Political and Economic Reforms in Eastern Europe and Latin America* (Cambridge: Cambridge University Press, 1991).

8. Elemer Hankiss: senior fellow at the Institute of Sociology of the Hugarian Academy of Sciences, Budapest.

9. MBB: Messerschmitt-Bölkow-Blohm, the enormous Munich-based defense and aerospace conglomerate.

10. Leipzig and Wenzelplatz: sites of the mass demonstrations that brought down the governments of East Germany and Czechoslovakia.

11. PDS: Party of Democratic Socialism, successor to the East German SED after the latter was dismantled in December 1989.

WHAT THEORIES CAN ACCOMPLISH – AND WHAT THEY CAN'T

1. The Federal Constitutional Court decreed separate East and West electoral areas for the December 1990 all-Germany *Bundestag* elections, as a way of checking the dominance of the Federal Republic's political parties in the former East Germany.

2. 'Return before compensation': principle according to which the return of the original owner, rather than a monetary settlement, is to have priority in settling outstanding claims for restitution of goods and property in the former East Germany.

3. Niklas Luhmann: professor of political science at the University of Bielefeld.

THE ASYLUM DEBATE

1. In the wake of German unification, the issue of political asylum became, apart from economic issues, the most contentious problem on the federal level to emerge in the expanded Federal Republic. Article 16 of the 1949 West German Basic Law stated simply that 'persons persecuted on political grounds shall enjoy the right of asylum.' Intended as a decisive historical negation of the mass forced emigrations and political persecutions of the Nazi dictatorship, Article 16 gave the Federal Republic the world's most open and unrestrictive asylum policy – and constituted a peculiar counterpart to the absence of any laws establishing the possibility of legal immigration and naturalization. The great majority of asylum applications were denied before German unification as well as after. But the long delays (often years) in processing these applications, the federal government's responsibility to provide shelter and a small stipend to applicants during the processing period, and

the number of applicants who remained in Germany illegally after their applications had been denied, led many politicians to complain that Germany's liberal asylum policy was too costly to maintain. Over the last fifteen years, ten attempts to introduce constitutional checks on Article 16 were unsuccessful.

This situation was deeply exacerbated by the sharp rise in immigration from eastern European countries as a result of the collapse of the Soviet bloc. Between 1989 and 1990, the rate of new asylum applications in the Federal Republic increased by 59 percent, with 193,000 in 1990 alone, more than three times the rate of any other European country during the same period. While less than 5 percent of these applicants were granted political asylum, the conservative CDU-CSU coalition began to issue calls for the revamping of asylum rights. In August of 1991, then-interior minister Wolfgang Schäuble declared that Germany's eastern border should be closed to asylum seekers from eastern Europe. A month later saw the first meeting between the ruling CDU/CSU/FDP coalition and the opposition SPD – which was opposed to constitutional changes – to negotiate amending existing asylum laws. By October 1991, in negotiations with the SPD, CDU representatives introduced a reformed asylum policy meant to curb the influx of new refugees. Its cornerstones – criticized as a cynical and strategic practical elimination of individual asylum rights by many in the opposition – consisted first in the federal government's self-arrogated right to compose lists of countries [*Länderliste*] in which, in the view of the federal government, citizens were not politically persecuted. Such lists would automatically rule out the possibility of political asylum for refugees from those nations, who could then legally be refused entry at the German border. Second, the CDU plan called for the automatic refusal of all asylum applicants who sought entry into the Federal Republic by way of so-called 'secure third states,' that is, states in which the Geneva Convention regarding refugees was in effect. Since every state on the Federal Republic's border – and particularly those on its eastern border, Austria, Poland, and the Czech Republic – qualified as 'secure third states,' this provision effectively eliminated the possibility of overland immigration by eastern European refugees.

By the summer of 1992, the SPD had gradually begun to drop its opposition to a constitutional change in Germany's asylum laws. In December 1992, all the major political parties agreed to an asylum compromise that retained the two cornerstones of the CDU plan, while providing refugees from civil war (e.g., those fleeing from the former Yugoslavia) a special right to remain in Germany independent of the issue of political asylum. In May 1993, amidst massive popular protests, the federal parliament approved amending the Federal Republic's Basic Law to adopt the new measures of the asylum compromise from the previous winter. In July 1993, the Federal Republic's new asylum law went into effect. The promise of individual asylum rights was stricken entirely from Article 16, to be restated verbatim in a new Article 16a. The conditions placed on individual asylum rights, specifically the 'lists of persecution-free countries' and the condition of not having entered from a 'secure third state,' were then recorded in the new Article 16a itself. In its first month, the new Article 16a reduced the number of new applications for political asylum in the Federal Republic by 34 percent.

2. Petersburger Turn: In November 1992, in a special meeting, the leadership of the SPD decided to reverse its position on two key political issues, bringing it in line with the conservative ruling coalition parties: it effectively surrendered its last opposition to a government-brokered constitutional change in asylum rights, as well as dropping its long-standing opposition to legal changes enabling the participation of German troops in UN peacekeeping operations. This change in key policies was widely regarded as a capitulation to pressure from the political right.

3. Franz Schönhuber: former SS officer and leader of the radical right-wing *Republikaner* party, which has gained considerable political mileage (and avoided being outlawed) by exploiting antiforeigner resentment and ethnic-nationalist furor while publicly denouncing violence against foreigners.

4. In November 1992, a firebomb attack by right-wing radicals on a house in the town of Mölln killed a Turkish woman and two young girls.

5. 'German Autumn: political and social crisis in autumn of 1977, provoked by radical left-wing terrorism.

6. Rudolph Seiters: prominent CDU politician and former Interior Minister; one of the strongest proponents of restrictions of asylum rights. Seiters resigned as Interior Minister in July 1993 in the wake of allegations of governmental mismanagement in the killing of a suspected left-wing terrorist by federal police agents.

7. 'Call back into history': reference to an influential book by this name. See Karl-Heinz Weissmann, *Rückruf in die Geschichte*, Berlin, 1992.

8. 'Boys at the *feuilleton*': Reference to the editors of the influential cultural magazine section of the conservative daily *Frankfurter Allgemeine Zeitung*.

AFTERWORD

1. Wolfgang Schäuble: CDU politician, former interior minister, and CDU leader in the federal parliament. Volker Rühe: CDU politician and defense minister.

2. Klaus Kinkel: foreign minister and leader of the junior coalition partner FDP party. *Plisch und Plum* were irritatingly cute twin cartoon teddy bears; the term was used derisively to refer to the cooperation of CSU finance minister Franz Josef Strauss and SDP economics minister Karl Schilling during the CDU/CSU-SDP 'grand coalition' of 1966–1969.

3. Solidarity pact: Since the earliest days of the unified Germany, economic problems – above all, the enormous economic disparities between the former West and East Germany – occasioned calls for a broad-based governmental arrangement on fiscal policies to finance the enormous costs of unification. This so-called 'solidarity pact' was the object of months of political wrangling. By March 1993, a compromise measure was agreed on by the political parties; deferring new personal taxes until 1995, the pact imposes a 7.5 percent 'solidarity surcharge' on incomes without calling for cuts in social spending.

4. Transportation Minister Günther Krause resigned in May 1993 amidst allegations of misuse of government funds.

5. 'What's Left': punning title of a series of articles on the future of the German left in the conservative *Frankfurter Allgemeine Zeitung*.

Index

Index